The Cybersecurity Career Compass

Your Guide from Campus to CISO

The Skills, Mindset, and Strategy to Succeed in Cybersecurity

Ashish Chugh

ISBN: 978-93-344-3303-6

DEDICATION

To every student, career changer, and quiet genius who asked, "Where do I fit?", this compass was built for you.

ACKNOWLEDGMENTS

This book is the culmination of countless conversations, mentorships, and moments of doubt that have been transformed into clarity. Thank you to the educators who inspire, the practitioners who lead with empathy, and the readers who challenge the status quo.

PREFACE

When I first entered the world of cybersecurity, I was overwhelmed, not by the threats themselves, but by the ambiguity surrounding them. Job titles blurred together. Certifications felt like alphabet soup. And every conversation seemed to start mid-sentence, assuming you already knew the jargon, the hierarchy, and the hidden rules.

This book was born from that disorientation and from the hundreds of conversations I've had since with students, career changers, and quiet geniuses who asked the same question: Where do I fit?

The Cybersecurity Career Compass is my answer. It's not a technical manual. It's a strategic guide, a mentorship-in-a-book, and a mirror held up to your strengths. It's designed to help you chart your course, choose your path, and move from theory to impact, whether you're a Builder, Detective, Strategist, or Tester.

You'll find practical tools here: resume frameworks, certification ladders, and recruiter insights. But you'll also find emotional intelligence, storytelling, and influence, because cybersecurity isn't just about defending systems. It's about navigating people, purpose, and power.

This book is for the unsure student, the career changer who's curious, and the practitioner who's ready to lead. It's for the educator who wants to guide with clarity, and the hiring manager who wants to build diverse, resilient teams.

It's for you.

Let's chart your course.

, Ashish Chugh

INTRODUCTION

Why Cybersecurity Needs a Compass, And Why You're Holding One
Cybersecurity is no longer a niche. It's a necessity. Every industry, every country, every digital interaction depends on it. And yet, for those trying to enter the field, the path is anything but clear.

You've probably heard the advice: "Get certified." "Learn to code." "Apply for SOC roles." But what if you're unsure which certification aligns with your goals? What if coding isn't your strength? What if you don't even know what a SOC is?

That's where this book comes in.

The Cybersecurity Career Compass is designed to help you:

- Understand the cybersecurity landscape without jargon or gatekeeping
- Identify your strengths through four personas: Builder, Detective, Strategist, Tester
- Explore real-world career paths across Offensive, Defensive, GRC, and Engineering domains
- Build your portfolio, prepare for interviews, and develop the soft skills that set leaders apart
- Navigate global job markets and contribute to inclusive, resilient teams

This isn't just a career guide. It's a strategic toolkit. You'll find Action Stations to help you reflect and plan, recruiter insights to decode hiring signals, and emotional intelligence frameworks to help you lead with empathy and influence.

Whether you're a student, a career changer, or a rising practitioner, this book is your map. But more importantly, it's your permission slip to explore, to question, and to lead.

Let's begin.

LEARNER PROFILES: WHO IS THIS BOOK FOR?

This book is a mentor in print for anyone ready to build or accelerate a career in cybersecurity.

- **Students & Aspiring Professionals**: For high school, college, and university students needing a clear and actionable plan to enter the cybersecurity field.
- **Career Changers**: For professionals from IT, law, business, and other fields seeking a proven roadmap to translate their existing experience into a successful cybersecurity career.
- **Graduates & First-Time Job Seekers**: For those looking for a competitive edge, with practical strategies to craft a standout resume, ace interviews, and land their first role.
- **Early-Career Practitioners**: For SOC analysts, junior engineers, and support staff who want to advance beyond their initial role by mastering the soft skills, branding, and strategic thinking that get you promoted.
- **Educators & Mentors**: For instructors and leaders who need a structured resource to guide their students and mentees from foundational concepts to professional excellence.
- **Ambitious Practitioners & Future Leaders**: For any security professional with their eyes on the prize: accelerating their journey from practitioner to influencer, visionary, and leader.

CONTENTS

1	THE DAY THE DIGITAL NATION WENT DARK	9
2	WHY CHOOSE CYBERSECURITY? (HINT: IT'S NOT JUST ABOUT THE HOODIE)	13
3	THE THREE PILLARS OF CYBER: AN OVERVIEW OF THE LANDSCAPE	18
4	THE OFFENSIVE PATH: ETHICAL HACKING AND PENETRATION TESTING	32
5	THE DEFENSIVE PATH: SECURITY OPERATIONS AND INCIDENT RESPONSE	39
6	THE STRATEGIST'S PATH: RISK, COMPLIANCE, AND GOVERNANCE (GRC)	47
7	THE BUILDER'S PATH: SECURITY ENGINEERING AND ARCHITECTURE	54
8	BEYOND THE KEYBOARD: BUILDING YOUR PERSONAL BRAND AND INFLUENCE	61
9	THE LAUNCH SEQUENCE: NAILING THE INTERVIEW AND LANDING THE ROLE	65
10	THE LONG GAME: FROM LEARNING TO LEADING	69
11	APPENDIX A: THE GLOBAL CYBER MARKET: A GUIDE TO INTERNATIONAL JOB HUBS	73
12	APPENDIX B: THRIVING IN A REMOTE-FIRST WORLD: TIPS FOR REMOTE WORK SUCCESS	77
13	APPENDIX C: A SPOTLIGHT ON DIVERSITY, EQUITY, AND INCLUSION (DEI) IN CYBER	81
14	APPENDIX D: THE ULTIMATE RESOURCE LIST: CURATED BLOGS, PODCASTS, AND CONFERENCES	85
15	APPENDIX E: THE GLOSSARY OF KEY TERMS	88
16	APPENDIX F: QUICK-REFERENCE GUIDE TO ROLES AND CERTIFICATIONS	96
17	ABOUT THE AUTHOR	98

1 THE DAY THE DIGITAL NATION WENT DARK

In the spring of 2007, Estonia was the future. A small Baltic nation renowned for its post-Soviet technological leap, it had quickly and enthusiastically embraced the internet like no other. Citizens voted online, filed taxes in minutes, and carried national ID cards that were smart cards. Every aspect of life, from banking to health to government communications, was integrated into a single, sophisticated system of digital efficiency. While other countries debated the wisdom of bold digitalization, Estonia charged ahead, becoming the world's first digital nation.

And then, in late April, the future began to flicker.

It started subtly. The websites of political parties and news outlets began to lag, then crash. For most citizens, it was an inconvenience, perhaps the result of heavy traffic or a technical glitch no different than a jammed phone line. But the disruptions escalated swiftly and relentlessly. Within hours, the websites for the President, Parliament, and nearly every government ministry were forced offline. Public services became inaccessible, communications snapped, and panic began to spread. The backbone of Estonian society was under attack.

Behind the scenes, government engineers and IT teams worked around the clock. They quickly realized this was not a simple malfunction: it was a sophisticated, coordinated deluge of digital traffic, flooding servers from a web of compromised computers across multiple countries. The term "Distributed Denial-of-Service Attack" (DDoS), once technical jargon for cybersecurity experts, became headline news for every citizen.

For three weeks, Estonia was under siege. Nothing felt safe or certain. The country's largest banks struggled to operate, and day-to-day transactions stalled; ATMs flashed error messages. News organizations, unable to update their websites, lost their ability to inform and reassure the public. Schools faced disruption, healthcare services slowed, and government officials scrambled to communicate. The digital infrastructure that provided so much convenience had become a weapon wielded against its very creators.

Few events in modern history had so starkly revealed the vulnerabilities of a connected society. Without a single soldier crossing its borders, without a shot being fired, Estonia, a pioneer of the digital age, was paralyzed by invisible adversaries using lines of code. Trust, convenience, and progress now came with unforeseen risks. The world watched, stunned, as a nation was brought to its knees not by tanks or warships, but by the silent force of cyberspace.

A New Definition for a New Reality

This was the moment the world awoke to a new era, one in which the boundaries of conflict shifted from land and sea to servers and routers. For centuries, power had depended on geography, including borders, armies, and access to vital resources. Now, a keyboard could disrupt commerce, cripple infrastructure, and silence institutions more effectively than any blockade. You are preparing to enter this world, a landscape where cybersecurity is not merely about protecting computers but about defending the backbone of our digital lives. Information security is the practice of ensuring the resilience and trustworthiness of our interconnected world. It is, in essence, the discipline devoted to safeguarding the digital nervous system of modern society.

Consider everything that moves across these networks: financial transactions that dictate prosperity, healthcare records that save lives, the supply chains that stock stores and deliver essentials, private messages that connect loved ones, and operational commands that keep hospitals running and ensure water flows to our cities. Each piece of data, each system, is both a marvel of human progress and a potential point of vulnerability.

In this field, professionals serve as architects who design secure systems, guardians who monitor threats, emergency responders who restore order after incidents, and translators who help society understand and manage risk. Their work touches every sector and every citizen, even those who never fully grasp its importance until it's threatened.

The Interconnected Ecosystem

Estonia's lessons resonate across the globe. There are no "tech companies". There are only companies that run on technology. The local bakery relies on cloud-based ordering platforms and digital payments. Global shippers coordinate fleets by using tracking software that processes millions of data points each minute. Hospitals stitch together patient care using complex webs of software, sensors, and remote diagnostic tools.

The extraordinary efficiency offered by deep digital integration comes at a price: fragility. A single flaw in a widely used component might ripple outwards, freezing operations and intimidating even the most prepared organizations. Many organizations learned that integrating technology is not enough. Understanding, securing, and adapting those systems is essential for survival.

A security breach today can have physical consequences tomorrow: surgeries may be delayed, flights may be canceled, supply chains may be disrupted, and economies may be affected. This reality propels cybersecurity out of the basement server room and into the boardroom. Security decisions impact strategy, brand reputation, regulatory compliance, and even national security. Leaders now ask: How resilient is our organization to invisible threats? Who is protecting the future we depend on?

Why Your Role Matters, Now More Than Ever

The digital economy is poised to shape the next century. New careers, industries, and even social structures will emerge and fade with the advent of technological waves. As a cybersecurity professional, your choices, vigilance, and creativity can literally help prevent crises and protect people, institutions, and entire communities.

But cybersecurity is not just a technical race. No single product or protocol can "solve" risk. True impact requires something deeper:

- Critical thinking and curiosity to spot and solve problems no one has seen before.
- Relationship-building and communication skills to persuade others to champion security in their team or organization.
- Vision and adaptability to steer through challenges that evolve faster than any textbook.
- Integrity and responsibility to manage sensitive data, protect privacy, and earn the trust others place in you.

Your Journey into This New Frontier

This book is designed to be your companion and guide on this journey. We will move beyond the technical manuals, beyond the rote memorization of certification guides. You will receive a strategic compass, a mentor in print. Inside, you'll find illuminating career spotlights with real professionals, candid insights from recruiters, and hands-on "Action Stations" to build your roadmap and mindset.

We'll explore the major cybersecurity vocations: the proactive testers (who think like attackers to prevent disaster before it strikes), the vigilant defenders (who watch and respond in real time), the strategic planners (who map out and govern risk), and the innovative builders (who design new systems and protocols from the ground up). Along the way, we'll highlight the skills most in demand —not just technical knowledge, but also critical thinking, communication, and business fluency.

A Place for Every Background and Every Strength

This is a domain that needs every kind of thinker, communicator, and problem solver. The digital frontier needs pioneers, not just those with technical brilliance, but also those with insatiable curiosity, diverse backgrounds, and the drive to solve meaningful problems. Whether you are a student staring at your graduation date, a seasoned professional considering a pivot, or fascinated by digital systems, you have opportunities to make a profound difference.
Imagine a world where your expertise could help a hospital avoid downtime, where your persuasion skills win your company's investment in a new security initiative, where your insight prevents fraud in a financial network, or where your leadership turns a crisis into an opportunity for growth. Cybersecurity is not merely a job; it's a mission —a chance to serve and protect in the virtual realm where so much of our future unfolds.

So, as you step into the pages ahead, begin with one central belief: your journey matters, and the future of cybersecurity needs your unique perspective and skills.

Let's chart your course together.

The only question left is: Are you ready to be one of the pioneers who will secure our digital future?

2 WHY CHOOSE CYBERSECURITY? (HINT: IT'S NOT JUST ABOUT THE HOODIE)

Close your eyes for a moment and picture a "cybersecurity expert."

For most people, the image comes straight from a movie poster: a lone figure in a darkened room, face illuminated by the glow of a screen filled with cascading green text. The hoodie is up, headphones are on, and with a few furious keystrokes, they can bring down empires or save the world. It's a compelling and mysterious image of an antisocial genius.

But, as you'll soon see, that cinematic stereotype is nearly pure fiction.

While a shadowy hacker might represent a tiny sliver of the offensive-security world, it misses the vast, collaborative, deeply human reality of the profession. Most information security work takes place in well-lit offices and lively video meetings; there's far more teamwork, communication, and strategy than there is "lone wolf" code-breaking.

"I never imagined my psychology degree would help fight cybercrime," says Priya, a Security Awareness Manager, "but understanding how people think helps me train them to spot scams and avoid risky clicks every single day."

Cybersecurity is less about lone geniuses; it's driven by teams of determined problem-solvers working together toward a shared mission: protecting the digital fabric of our society.

The real question isn't whether you fit a Hollywood cliché. It's whether you have the curiosity, drive, empathy, and desire to find your place in one of the most stable, diverse, and impactful professions of the 21st century. And the world has never needed people like you more.

The Opportunity Gulf: A World in Urgent Need

Imagine a mid-sized hospital in a growing city. Its administrators have just invested heavily in new diagnostic machines, digital patient records, and telemedicine services. They're providing better care than ever, but their small IT team is struggling to keep up. The hospital's director reads headlines about ransomware attacks crippling healthcare providers and knows the hospital is a prime target. She posts a job opening for a qualified security analyst. Weeks go by, then months. Only a handful of candidates apply, usually lacking the right skills or quickly hired by larger firms for higher salaries. The hospital remains vulnerable, and the position remains unfilled.

This reality plays out worldwide, not just in healthcare but across every industry. Headlines scream about breaches and attacks, but the bigger story is the staggering shortage of defenders. The gap between the demand for skilled professionals and the available talent has reached a critical point.

- **Data Spotlight**: The Global Workforce Gap
- **Source**: The $(ISC)^2$ Cybersecurity Workforce Study. This annual report surveys thousands of cybersecurity professionals worldwide to gauge the current state of the industry.
- **The Data**: The 2023 report found that the global cybersecurity workforce gap had grown to a record 4 million professionals. This means there are 4 million needed positions for which no skilled person is available to hire.
- **Reference Link**: The full report is available at the $(ISC)^2$ official website: https://www.isc2.org/research/workforce-study

In India, the situation is equally critical, with the nation's technology sector forecasting a significant need for security talent.

- **Data Spotlight**: The Workforce Demand in India
- **Source**: NASSCOM (National Association of Software and Service Companies) and the Data Security Council of India (DSCI).
- **The Data**: In reports from the early 2020s, NASSCOM and DSCI began projecting that India's cybersecurity workforce would need to grow to more than 1 million professionals by 2025 to meet the demands of the rapidly growing digital economy. (Source: Cyber Security Scope in India - Bangalore)
- **Reference Link**: This widely cited forecast is discussed in major Indian publications, such as The Economic Times.

For you, this gap represents an unmatched opportunity: job security in turbulent times, a market where your skills aren't just wanted; they're desperately needed. You'll enter a field where, from day one, you're an essential member of the team, not just another cog in the machine.

Finding Your Place: The Four Cyber Personas

Because cybersecurity is vast, there's no single "type" of security professional. Your unique strengths, whether in problem-solving, planning, creativity, collaboration, or empathy, have a place here.

Let's move beyond the hoodie and meet the four core personas that shape security teams everywhere:

1. The Detective (Digital Forensics & Incident Response)

When alarms go off, the Detective rushes to the scene. Their work begins after a breach, much as a crime scene investigator would. They meticulously collect and analyze evidence, such as log files, malware, and digital traces, to reconstruct what happened and prevent future incidents.

- **Drives**: Passion for solving puzzles, attention to detail, calm under pressure.
- **Roles**: Digital Forensics Analyst, Incident Responder, Threat Intelligence Analyst.

"After our hospital's ransomware scare, I spent three days reconstructing every move the attackers made. It was a puzzle only teamwork could solve." — Anjali, Incident Responder.

2. The Builder (Security Engineering & Architecture)

Builders create the defenses that protect organizations from disaster. They design robust systems, from networks to cloud infrastructure, embedding security in every layer. Their focus is on anticipating threats, building resilience, and empowering teams.

- **Drives:** Love for creating, desire for resilience, proactive mindset.
- **Roles**: Security Engineer, Cloud Security Architect, Application Security Specialist.

"Nothing feels better than seeing a system hold up against an attack I prepared for and knowing I helped keep thousands of families safe." — Ahmed, Cloud Security Engineer.

3. The Strategist (Governance, Risk & Compliance (GRC))

Strategists connect technology, business, and people. Instead of configuring firewalls, they design the policies and culture that keep organizations safe. They analyze risks, guide informed decisions, and empower employees to be the first line of defense.

- **Drives**: Big-picture focus, communication, persuasion, understanding human behavior.
- **Roles**: Risk Analyst, Compliance Manager, Security Awareness Manager.

"My role isn't about tech. It's about translating risk into real decisions that leaders understand. Sometimes, saving the day is about what you say." — Priya, Security Awareness Manager.

4. The Tester (Penetration Testing & Offensive Security)

Testers are ethical hackers, paid to think like adversaries. They probe systems to expose hidden vulnerabilities before real attackers can exploit them. Creativity, curiosity, and determination drive them to unmask and fix every flaw.

- **Drives**: Curiosity, competitiveness, creative problem-solving.
- **Roles**: Penetration Tester, Red Teamer, Vulnerability Researcher.

"Success? Finding a flaw in a payments app before millions of users are exposed. You're the hero, but no one ever suspects you!" — Ramesh, Penetration Tester.

A Vocation of Impact

Cybersecurity professionals make a real difference, often in ways that go unnoticed until disaster is averted. The detective's forensic work exposes global fraud rings; the builder's secure network design keeps vital services running; the strategist's training helps staff stop phishing attacks; and the tester's discoveries protect millions from financial loss.

In this field, soft skills, such as listening, teaching, teamwork, and storytelling, matter just as much as technical expertise. Most security pros spend their day working with people, not just code.

The Rewards: Growth, Stability, and Purpose

Information security is both meaningful and practical. Entry-level salaries are among the best in tech, often more than double the average for new graduates, and rise quickly with experience.

More importantly, the rapid evolution of threats guarantees lifelong learning and growth. You likely won't be in the same role for long. Dedication and curiosity can accelerate you from analyst to leader, or even to boardroom advisor, far faster than most industries.

A 2024 (ISC)² survey found that 75% of CISOs had begun as analysts within the past decade. This is a field that invests in its own: curiosity is rewarded, and growth is built in.

Action Station: Find Your Compass Point

You've just met the four personas that drive cybersecurity teams.

Which one feels closest to you? There's no wrong answer; recognizing your strengths is the first step in your own career adventure.

Take a moment. In a few sentences, describe why being a Builder, Detective, Strategist, or Tester excites you. What about that role that matches your interests, skills, or values?

Hold onto that answer; it's the first official reading on your career compass. In the next chapters, we'll begin exploring the map.

3 THE THREE PILLARS OF CYBER: AN OVERVIEW OF THE LANDSCAPE

Standing at the edge of the cybersecurity world, it's easy to be overwhelmed. SOCs, SIEMs, GRC, AppSec, Red & Blue Teams, CTI acronyms, and job titles flood the landscape, making it difficult to see the path ahead. But with a simple map, the terrain becomes clear.

To understand the profession, let's use a timeless analogy, the defense of a medieval castle. In this kingdom, security depends on three distinct but interconnected groups. First are the Guardians (the Blue Team), the vigilant soldiers who patrol the walls and defend against daily threats. Second are the Testers (the Red Team), the elite specialists hired to think like the enemy and find weaknesses before a real attack. Finally, there is the Royal Council (the GRC team), the strategists who write the laws, manage the kingdom's resources, and decide what is most important to protect.

Nearly every cybersecurity role, tool, and strategy aligns with one of these three core pillars. This model provides our map. Now, let's meet the modern-day professionals who hold these critical positions and see what their work truly entails.

The First Pillar: Defensive Security (The Blue Team)

Inside the castle's towering walls, a network of guardians works together to keep intruders at bay and protect all the kingdom's assets. This is Defensive Security, the daily work of resilience, vigilance, and rapid response.

Cybersecurity demands constant vigilance, but that alone is not enough. Blue Team professionals must be as cunning as their adversaries. It's a contest of wits: defenders must outthink attackers at every turn. That means anticipating clever infiltration tactics, obsessively studying hacker psychology, and learning from Red Team simulations and threat intelligence. Attackers are creative and relentless; defenders are challenged to remain agile, perceptive, and smarter with every new day. If you can't outsmart the adversary, the whole kingdom pays the price.

Security Operations Center (SOC) Analyst

A Security Operations Center (SOC) Analyst is an information security professional responsible for detecting, analyzing, and responding to cyber threats and incidents within an organization's IT environment on a 24/7 basis. They are the frontline defenders, utilizing security technologies and threat intelligence to ensure continuous monitoring and rapid reaction to security events.

Key Responsibilities:

- Monitor security alerts and events in real-time using tools like a SIEM.
- Triage, investigate, and escalate potential security incidents.
- Perform initial incident response actions to contain threats.
- Generate reports on security events and trends for management.
- Maintain and tune security tools (e.g., SIEM and EDR/XDR) to optimize detection capabilities and reduce the volume of false positive alerts.
- Create and update security documentation, including alert playbooks, incident response procedures, and standard operating procedures (SOPs).

Imagine Priya in a modern SOC, surrounded by glowing screens tracking the health of thousands of endpoints, servers, and cloud resources. Her morning starts with reviewing the previous night's alerts: a failed login attempt, a sudden spike in outbound data, or an employee's device connecting from an unusual location. Her actions require strong technical knowledge, crisis management skills, precise communication, and constant collaboration with incident responders and forensic analysts.

Success here depends not only on speed and accuracy but also on teamwork and the ability to translate urgent technical findings into clear, actionable messages for managers, clients, and other departments. When the stakes are high, cross-functional collaboration can mean the difference between a minor incident and a major breach.

Network Security Engineer

A Network Security Engineer (NSE) is a specialized security professional responsible for designing, implementing, configuring, and maintaining the security infrastructure of an organization's computer networks. They focus on protecting the network perimeter and internal traffic from unauthorized access, disruption, and data breaches using technical controls and defense strategies.

Key Responsibilities:

- Design, deploy, and maintain firewalls, VPNs, and intrusion prevention systems.
- Monitor network traffic for anomalies and potential threats.

- Develop and enforce network security policies and procedures.
- Respond to network-related security incidents and vulnerabilities.
- Implement and manage network segmentation (e.g., VLANs, micro-segmentation) to minimize the blast radius of a breach.
- Conduct regular network penetration testing and vulnerability assessments to proactively identify and remediate weaknesses in the infrastructure before attackers exploit them.

Imagine Raj, responsible for the organization's firewalls and intrusion prevention systems. One afternoon, his deep curiosity leads him to investigate unusual traffic headed for a rarely used web server, revealing an attacker exploiting an old vulnerability. Raj coordinates a rapid response: patching the software, updating the firewall rules, and working with developers to close the loophole.

Beyond technical troubleshooting, Raj's effectiveness relies on his adaptability and clear communication, which facilitate meetings with developers, explain threats to executives, and update documentation for future training.

Digital Forensics Specialist

A Digital Forensics Specialist (DFS) is a highly specialized technical investigator responsible for identifying, collecting, preserving, analyzing, and reporting on digital evidence in a manner admissible in legal or internal disciplinary proceedings. They work to uncover the "who, what, when, where, and how" of a cyber-incident by meticulously examining data from various digital sources.

Key Responsibilities:

- Collect, preserve, and analyze digital evidence from computers, servers, and mobile devices.
- Reconstruct timelines of security incidents to identify attacker methods.
- Prepare detailed forensic reports for internal stakeholders or legal proceedings.
- Recover data from compromised or damaged systems.
- Maintain and validate forensic tools and laboratories to ensure consistency, accuracy, and compliance with industry standards and best practices (e.g., using write blockers).
- Provide expert testimony in court or during internal hearings to explain the findings, methodology, and integrity of the collected digital evidence.

When a breach occurs, Blue Team forensics experts become cyber detectives. Meera, a digital forensics analyst, reconstructs attacker activity by examining logs and device images. Her methodical reporting and clear translation of complex findings to legal and management teams often make the difference between catching an intruder and losing valuable data forever.

A successful Blue Team thrives on discipline, resilience, and teamwork, often under intense time pressure. Their diverse backgrounds and approaches strengthen defenses against a wide range of attacks.

The Second Pillar: Offensive Security (The Red Team)

Strong walls can breed a dangerous sense of security. Red Team professionals keep organizations humble and resilient by finding weaknesses before real criminals do. The Red Team represents the adversarial perspective; they are the authorized "attackers" who constantly challenge an organization's security controls to measure how prepared it is for a real-world breach.

The philosophy behind the Red Team is simple: assume a breach is inevitable.

Their Core Mission: The Adversarial Mindset

The Red Team's mission is not just to find individual vulnerabilities (like an outdated web application or a weak password); their goal is to test the entire security ecosystem, including:

- **Technology**: Can they bypass the firewall, confuse the monitoring software, or exfiltrate data undetected?
- **People**: Can they trick employees into revealing credentials (Social Engineering)?
- **Processes**: How quickly does the Security Operations Center (SOC) detect and respond to a sophisticated, multi-stage attack?

Red Teams often engage in "full-scope" campaigns that mimic real attackers. These campaigns include initial reconnaissance, gaining a foothold, moving laterally through the network, and achieving a pre-defined objective, such as retrieving a specific confidential document.

Bridging the "Sense of Security" Gap

By operating covertly and without the knowledge of the primary defense teams (the Blue Team), the Red Team forces the organization to perform under pressure. This directly addresses the "dangerous sense of security" by:

- **Measuring True Detection**: It reveals whether the SOC (Blue Team) can actually detect a nuanced threat, rather than just reacting to textbook alerts.

- **Validating Incident Response**: It tests the organization's Mean Time to Respond (MTTR) and validates whether containment and eradication procedures work in a stressful, real-time environment.
- **Prioritizing Remediation**: The findings deliver actionable, real-world data on which vulnerabilities represent the highest business risk, allowing security budgets and developer time to be spent where they matter most.

Penetration Tester

A Penetration Tester (Pen Tester) is a security expert hired to simulate an attack on an organization's systems, networks, applications, and cloud environments, with full authorization, to discover exploitable vulnerabilities and evaluate the organization's security posture before a real attacker does. The role requires a creative, adversarial mindset focused on demonstrating the real-world business risk posed by security flaws.

Key Responsibilities:

- Perform authorized security tests on networks, applications, and cloud infrastructure.
- Identify and exploit vulnerabilities to assess their real-world business impact.
- Document findings and provide clear, actionable remediation recommendations.
- Communicate complex technical risks to technical and non-technical audiences.
- Develop custom scripts, tools, or exploits to test unique or zero-day vulnerabilities in a target-specific environment, demonstrating advanced adversarial skill.
- Adhere to a strict 'Rules of Engagement' to ensure ethical conduct, legal compliance, and avoidance of any unintended damage or denial-of-service during testing activities.

Ramesh is hired to challenge a bank's new mobile app. For several weeks, he has been performing simulated attacks, discovering a function that could enable unauthorized account takeovers. His success depends not only on his technical skill but on his persuasive communication to convince developers and leaders of the business risk, ensuring his advice isn't ignored.

Continuous learning, attention to detail, and empathy (for both users and defenders) enable penetration testers to identify new risks as technology evolves.

Red Team Operator

A Red Team Operator is a cybersecurity specialist responsible for emulating sophisticated threat actors to test and enhance an organization's defense mechanisms. By simulating authentic attack techniques, Red Team Operators provide actionable insights into the organization's ability to detect, respond, and recover from real-world cyber threats. These professionals blend technical expertise, psychological insight, and creative problem-solving to reveal vulnerabilities across people, processes, and technology. Their work helps organizations proactively identify and remediate security weaknesses before malicious actors can exploit them.

Key Responsibilities:

- Develop and deploy custom tools and malware: Red Team Operators frequently build or adapt offensive security tools to evade detection and mimic current threat actors.
- Collaborate with Blue Team and Incident Response: Participate in debriefs and tabletop exercises to foster a culture of shared learning and continuous improvement.
- Document and maintain evidence: Maintain detailed attack paths, exploitation logs, and artifacts for post-operation analysis and regulatory requirements.
- Continuous learning and threat intelligence: Keep abreast of the latest adversary tactics, techniques, and procedures (TTPs) to ensure simulations are current and relevant.
- Ethical and legal compliance: Ensure all Red Team operations have written authorization and strictly adhere to legal/ethical boundaries.
- Simulate real-world adversary tactics in long-term campaigns.
- Test the organization's overall detection and response: people, process, and technology.
- Conduct reconnaissance, social engineering, and stealthy lateral network movement.
- Provide strategic reports to leadership.

Red Team operators like Sarah run "full-scope" exercises. For one client, she spends months gathering intelligence, custom-building malware, and probing every layer of their security. With stealth and ingenuity, her team demonstrates real-world risk, requiring immense creativity, adaptability, and understanding of organizational psychology.

Vulnerability Researcher

A Red Team Operator is a highly skilled offensive security specialist who conducts full-scope, multi-layered simulated attacks (known as Red Team Operations) to rigorously test an organization's overall resilience against real-world, sophisticated adversaries. Unlike a penetration tester who often focuses on finding and exploiting technical vulnerabilities in a limited scope, the Operator mimics a persistent threat actor to evaluate the organization's detection and response capabilities as a whole.

Key Responsibilities:

- Discover previously unknown ("zero-day") vulnerabilities in software, hardware, and protocols.
- Analyze and reverse-engineer code for exploitability.
- Responsibly disclose findings to vendors for patching.
- Publish research to boost community knowledge.
- Develop custom payloads and tooling (e.g., Command and Control or C2 frameworks, evasion techniques) to bypass existing security controls and remain undetected by standard defensive measures.
- Integrate findings into purple team exercises by collaborating with defenders (the Blue Team) post-operation to help them improve their alert rules and defensive TTPs.

Some Red Team specialists focus on discovering novel flaws. Alex, a researcher studying encryption libraries, uncovers a flaw in a router's firmware after months of intensive research. Passion, tenacity, and technical depth power these discoveries, which may protect millions before criminals can exploit them.

Red Team work demands not only technical mastery but also collaboration, innovation, and superb communication with Blue Teams and GRC when vulnerabilities are identified.

The Third Pillar: Governance, Risk & Compliance (GRC)

Security isn't just about technology. The castle's royal council sets priorities, enforces laws, and adapts strategy, turning technical defenses into business value.

Security is often viewed through a purely technical lens, such as firewalls, antivirus software, and encryption. However, these tools are expensive walls and moats if a clear **strategy, defined accountability, and adherence to laws (GRC)** are not in place. GRC is the management structure that ensures security technology is deployed effectively, aligned with business goals, and compliant with all legal and regulatory mandates.

1. Governance: The Royal Council's Mandate

Governance provides the **strategic direction, oversight, and accountability** for security within the organization. It's about setting the "laws of the land" that the security team must follow.

- **Strategic Alignment**: The primary role of governance is ensuring that security spending and priorities directly support the organization's mission and risk appetite. For example, if a company's main asset is its proprietary manufacturing design, governance mandates that maximum resources are allocated to protecting those intellectual property servers, even if other threats exist.
- **Defining Roles and Responsibilities**: Governance establishes who is responsible for what. It establishes committees (such as a Security Steering Committee) and defines the roles of the Board of Directors, C-suite, IT, and the rest of the workforce in maintaining security. This prevents key tasks from being overlooked.
- **Policy and Standard Setting**: This is where the security policy is created, the high-level document stating *what* the organization aims to protect and *how* it will manage risk. **Standards** and **procedures** then detail the technical and operational steps to achieve this (e.g., all laptops must use multi-factor authentication).

2. Risk Management: Assessing Threats to the Kingdom

Risk is the practice of systematically identifying, assessing, and treating threats to the business. It answers the question: "What bad things could happen, and how much would they cost us?"

- **Risk Identification and Assessment**: The organization continually scouts for vulnerabilities, assesses the likelihood of a threat event (like a data breach), and determines its potential business impact (financial, reputational, legal). This allows security efforts to be prioritized based on the most significant risks.
- **Risk Treatment (The Decision):** Once a risk is assessed, the organization must decide what to do:
    - **Mitigate:** Apply controls (e.g., encryption) to reduce the risk.
    - **Accept:** Acknowledge the risk and live with it (usually for low-impact or high-cost-to-fix risks).
    - **Transfer:** Shift the risk to a third party (e.g., purchasing cyber insurance).
    - **Avoid:** Change business practices to eliminate the risk altogether.
- **Continuous Monitoring:** Risk management isn't a one-time event. It

requires continuous feedback loops to track whether existing controls remain effective as the business environment (and threats) change.

3. Compliance: Adhering to the Law and the Charter

Compliance ensures the organization operates within the boundaries of external laws, regulations, contracts, and internal policies.

- **External Regulations:** This includes mandatory adherence to laws like the **GDPR** (for privacy), **HIPAA** (for healthcare data), or **PCI DSS** (for handling credit card data). Compliance measures translate these legal requirements into concrete security controls and audit checks.
- **Internal Policies and Contracts:** This ensures the organization adheres to its own security policies defined by Governance, as well as contractual agreements with clients and vendors regarding data protection.
- **Audit and Reporting:** Compliance requires frequent **audits** (internal and external) to verify that security controls are deployed correctly and functioning as required by law. The results are reported to the governing body (Board/C-suite) to prove due diligence.

The Value Proposition: Turning Cost into Business Value

By establishing the GRC framework, the organization achieves several critical business outcomes:

Outcome	Description
Accountability	Security failures are traced to a specific person, department, or process, preventing "security by committee" where no one is truly responsible.
Informed Decisions	Security is managed with a **business case**. Investment decisions are based on quantifiable risk reduction rather than fear.
Trust and Assurance	Demonstrating GRC maturity builds **trust** with customers, partners, and regulators, enabling the business to enter new markets or handle sensitive data.
Legal Protection	Compliance provides a crucial legal shield, proving the organization took "reasonable care" to protect data in the event of a breach or regulatory fine.

GRC Business Outcomes

Let's look at the roles in GRC.

Risk Manager

The Risk Manager's core function is to systematically manage uncertainty (risk) to protect the organization's assets and enable it to achieve its objectives. They bridge the gap between technical security teams and business leadership.

Key Responsibilities:

- Identify, assess, and quantify security risks across the organization.
- Maintain a risk register to track and prioritize threats.
- Advise on mitigation strategies and investments.
- Facilitate risk assessments and tabletop exercises.
- Collaborate with leadership and the Board to formally define the organization's Risk Appetite and Tolerance
- Ensure that security controls are not only implemented but are effective and correctly mapped to regulatory and legal requirements
- Act as the primary champion for risk awareness
- Integrate Risk Management with Incident Response
- Manage Vendor and Supply Chain Risk

Nidhi's job at a global financial firm is to ensure security investments align with actual threats. When privacy laws shift or a new cyber risk emerges, she guides the organization through scenario planning and analysis to ensure a proactive approach. Success depends on collaboration across IT, HR, and legal, as well as her ability to translate risk into plain language for decision-makers.

Compliance Analyst

A Compliance Analyst is responsible for ensuring that an organization operates within legal boundaries and adheres to regulatory requirements, industry standards, and internal policies. They serve as the bridge between complex regulatory frameworks and practical business operations, helping organizations avoid legal penalties, financial losses, and reputational damage. These professionals monitor regulatory changes, conduct audits, develop compliance programs, and provide guidance to various departments to maintain ethical and lawful business practices across all organizational activities.

Key Responsibilities:

- Develop and update compliance policies and procedures based on regulatory changes and business needs
- Create compliance training materials and conduct employee training sessions
- Perform risk assessments to identify compliance vulnerabilities and

potential exposure areas

- Monitor regulatory changes and assess their impact on organizational operations
- Maintain compliance monitoring systems and key performance indicators (KPIs)
- Prepare detailed compliance reports for senior management and regulatory bodies
- Document compliance findings, remediation efforts, and audit trails
- Maintain evidence collection for compliance verification and audit purposes
- Investigate compliance violations and develop corrective action plans
- Support cybersecurity incident response activities from a compliance perspective
- Coordinate breach notifications and regulatory disclosures when required
- Serve as subject matter expert on compliance matters for various departments
- Act as primary liaison with regulatory bodies and external auditors
- Provide compliance guidance to cross-functional teams and management
- Ensure adherence to legal, regulatory, and industry standards (e.g., HIPAA, PCI-DSS).
- Conduct internal audits and assessments.
- Coordinate with external auditors for certification.
- Translate compliance needs into technical and policy controls.

Ravi oversees whether technical teams, policies, and practices meet evolving external requirements. His role requires him to communicate technical nuances to non-technical teams, ensuring no one misunderstands the importance of compliance.

Security Awareness Program Manager

The Security Awareness Program Manager leads the strategy, development, and execution of organization-wide security awareness and training initiatives. This role is responsible for fostering a culture of security-first thinking and empowering employees to understand, identify, and respond effectively to evolving security threats. The manager designs engaging content and campaigns tailored for diverse roles, partners with GRC (Governance, Risk, and Compliance) and IT security teams, and measures impact through robust behavioral metrics and feedback cycles. The ultimate goal: embed security as a daily habit and shared responsibility across the enterprise.

Key Responsibilities:

- Align programs with overall GRC and regulatory requirements (e.g., ISO 27001, NIST, GDPR), collaborating closely with compliance teams.
- Continuously assess the effectiveness of training through data-driven metrics, incident feedback, and employee testing.
- Tailor awareness content for audience needs, e.g., executives, new hires, technical staff, and non-technical teams.
- Integrate lessons from security incidents to adapt and refine awareness content.
- Work with HR, IT, and legal teams to ensure onboarding, offboarding, and policy changes remain supported by security education.
- Champion diversity and inclusion in security training, making content accessible and relatable to all roles and backgrounds.
- Stay current with industry threats and best practices, updating content as cyber risks and technologies evolve.Develop and deliver training across the organization.
- Design simulated phishing campaigns to build employee vigilance.
- Communicate best practices in engaging, clear formats.
- Report on awareness and behavioral improvements.

Rekha builds a culture where every employee feels responsible for security. She adapts lessons for diverse roles and backgrounds, turning security into an everyday habit.

GRC teams are strongest when they reflect the organization's diversity, adaptability, and broad skill sets, turning complexity into consensus and strategy into scalable action.

Unity in Action: A Real-World Scenario

Picture a critical vulnerability being discovered in widely used software, a "zero-day" threat. The pillars unite:

- **GRC**: Immediately assesses business risk, communicates with leadership about potential impacts, and coordinates the official response.
- **Blue Team**: Applies patches as they become available, while SOC analysts hunt for exploitation attempts. Collaboration across teams ensures rapid mitigation and good documentation.
- **Red Team**: Replicates attackers' techniques and tests the effectiveness of Blue Team fixes, providing vital feedback to further hone detection and defense.

A global ransomware campaign targeted a financial institution. Thanks to Red Team exercises that exposed weaknesses, the Blue Team's rapid detection and response, and GRC's updated emergency plans, they blocked the attack in real time, saving millions and protecting customer trust.

Throughout, communication between pillars (technical, business, and legal) was essential. Diversity in the team's backgrounds and perspectives made the response more resilient and innovative.

Skills That Keep the Castle Strong

Security demands more than technical excellence. It's built on:

- **Collaboration**: across technical and non-technical teams. Effective security is not limited to the domain of IT or cybersecurity professionals. It requires active collaboration between all departments, from HR, legal, and operations, to executive leadership and customer-facing teams. This ensures that security practices integrate into workflows, address real-world business needs, and leverage shared expertise. For example, HR might help spot suspicious employee behavior, while legal helps ensure compliance with privacy laws. Joint incident response planning, cross-team tabletop exercises, and shared risk assessments foster a united, organization-wide defense.
- **Communication**: clarity with details and strategy alike. Security strategies and technical controls must be clearly communicated, not just in technical jargon, but in accessible, actionable messages for all audiences. This means explaining the "why" and "how" behind policies, incident plans, or detected threats so every stakeholder understands their role. Senior managers need big-picture strategy; frontline employees require crisp guidance on daily practices. High-quality communication bridges gaps, prevents misunderstandings, and ensures swift, coordinated responses in emergencies.
- **Adaptability**: responding quickly to new threats and regulations that emerge. Cyber risk is constantly evolving. Attackers develop fresh techniques, while regulators introduce new standards faster than ever. A strong security program embraces change, rapidly retires obsolete controls, adopts innovative defensive practices, and revises processes to stay compliant. Adaptability means running regular threat intelligence reviews, updating training, refining controls after incidents, and remaining proactive rather than reactive.
- **Curiosity**: never settling, always asking "What if?". The best defenders maintain a mindset of continuous inquiry. Curiosity drives penetration testing, post-mortem analysis of breaches, and "what if" scenario planning that uncovers overlooked risks. It inspires security teams to test assumptions, question why processes exist, try new tools, research

external threats, and understand the attacker's perspective. Curiosity transforms static policies into living safeguards that anticipate emerging challenges.

- **Vigilance**: the relentless readiness to spot and outsmart increasingly cunning attackers. Security is a 24/7 responsibility; threats may surface anytime, anywhere, often disguised or highly persistent. Vigilant security teams and employees consistently monitor systems, scrutinize anomalies, and verify the legitimacy of emails, downloads, or requests. Vigilance combines automated detection tools with human intuition: a security-aware workforce can often spot subtle social engineering tactics that machines miss.
- **Inclusion**: drawing on diverse perspectives and skill sets for greater strength. Today's attackers exploit cultural, linguistic, and behavioral nuances. By building inclusive teams with diverse backgrounds, experiences, and expertise, organizations can anticipate and counter a broader range of threats. Inclusion brings broader knowledge, technical, legal, psychological, and fresh ideas to problem-solving. It also ensures that security messaging, training, and controls reach and resonate across the entire organization, maximizing engagement and effectiveness.

Action Station: Map Your Cyber Castle

Draw your own castle diagram. List out the Blue Team guardians (SOC Analyst, Network Security Engineer, Digital Forensics Specialist), the Red Team testers (Penetration Tester, Red Team Operator, Vulnerability Researcher), and the GRC strategists (Risk Manager, Compliance Analyst, Security Awareness Manager).

Think about three cybersecurity jobs you've heard of: Where do they fit?

Finally, reflect: Which pillar draws you most? What skills and interests might help you succeed there? And how would you outsmart adversaries to protect your own "kingdom"?

Understanding these pillars transforms the overwhelming world of cybersecurity into a clear, navigable map, one you can use to chart your own path to a resilient and rewarding digital career.

4 THE OFFENSIVE PATH: ETHICAL HACKING AND PENETRATION TESTING

While some are driven to build taller walls and stronger gates, others are irresistibly drawn to finding a way over, under, or through them. This is the essence of the offensive security mindset, not about destruction, but about discovery. Offensive security is creative, rigorous quality control, driven by the belief that the only way to build resilient defense is to test it as expertly and inventively as real-world adversaries would.

This is the world of ethical hacking, where "ethical" is the most important word. Professionals on this path operate with a strict code of conduct and explicit permission, working with defenders, not against them. This collaborative spirit is at the core of the profession; the most successful offensive security professionals blend technical mastery with teamwork, integrity, and the ability to learn and communicate effectively across diverse audiences. They are industry "troubleshooters," hired to help organizations patch weaknesses before malicious actors can exploit them, ultimately creating a safer digital ecosystem for everyone.

Let's explore the key roles that define this exciting path.

The Roles of the Offensive Path

Let's look at the roles of the offensive path.

Penetration Tester

The Penetration Tester, or "pentester," is the most common role in offensive security. Versatile specialists hired to give organizations a focused, practical assessment, they work intensively over a set period, often one to three weeks, to find vulnerabilities and produce clear, actionable advice. Success relies not just on finding flaws, but on explaining them to people who may be hearing about such risks for the first time. Top pentesters excel at clear communication, empathy for developers, and professionalism in client partnerships.

Key Responsibilities:

- Perform social engineering assessments (phishing, vishing, USB drops) and physical security tests to evaluate the human and facility elements.
- Develop and refine custom scripts, attack methodologies, and test

plans for each assessment.

- Research and stay current with new exploits, attack vectors, and security trends; continuously learn and update methodologies.
- Perform code review for security vulnerabilities in applications where applicable.
- Present findings to both technical audiences and executives, tailoring risk communication to different levels of understanding.
- Assist remediation by providing technical support and retesting resolved vulnerabilities.
- Document and maintain evidence and logs throughout the assessment for accountability and regulatory needs.
- Adhere to legal, ethical, and contractual obligations at all times.
- Plan and scope security testing engagements with clients (defining "rules of engagement" and trust).
- Conduct network, web application, and cloud infrastructure penetration tests.
- Identify, validate, and (safely) exploit vulnerabilities using both tools and manual ingenuity.
- Write detailed, professional reports explaining technical discoveries, business risks, and specific remediation steps.

The Penetration Tester, or "pentester," is the most common role in offensive security. Versatile specialists hired to give organizations a focused, practical assessment, they work intensively over a set period, often one to three weeks, to find vulnerabilities and produce clear, actionable advice. Success relies not just on finding flaws, but on explaining them to people who may be hearing about such risks for the first time. Top pentesters excel at clear communication, empathy for developers, and professionalism in client partnerships.

Application Security (AppSec) Specialist

An Application Security Specialist is a cybersecurity expert dedicated to safeguarding software applications, web, mobile, and cloud, from design through development and deployment. Embedded within development teams, AppSec specialists promote a *DevSecOps* philosophy, ensuring security is integrated at every stage of the Software Development Life Cycle (SDLC). They possess strong software engineering backgrounds and apply industry-leading standards, threat modeling, and hands-on testing to proactively identify and mitigate vulnerabilities.

AppSec specialists partner with developers, architects, and product managers to translate business and technical requirements into secure design patterns. They manage vulnerability intake from automated tools and bug bounty programs, educate teams on secure coding, and build cultures of shared responsibility through clear guidance and toolsets.

Key Responsibilities:

- Analyze application architecture to proactively identify potential attack vectors and prioritize remediation.
- Integrate security tooling (SAST, DAST, SCA, IAST) and automate repeatable processes in CI/CD pipelines.
- Support post-incident investigations, root cause analysis, and help teams recover securely.
- Ensure applications meet legal frameworks (PCI, GDPR, HIPAA), helping dev teams align with policies.
- Track and report application security maturity, trends, and improvement areas to leadership.
- Stay updated on evolving threats, standards (OWASP Top Ten), and disseminate knowledge to teams.
- Perform security code reviews and dynamic testing for web and mobile apps.
- Work directly with development teams to bake security into the software creation process (DevSecOps).
- Develop and maintain code standards, guide engineers, and foster a culture of shared responsibility.
- Triage vulnerability reports from automated tools and public bug bounty programs.

While a pentester often attacks applications from the outside, an AppSec specialist is often embedded within development teams, fluent in software engineering, security best practices, and cross-team collaboration. AppSec specialists model proactive partnership: they educate, translate business needs into secure code, and ensure that security is never an afterthought.

Red Teamer

A Red Teamer emulates advanced, real-world threat actors by conducting covert, objective-driven engagements that challenge the full breadth of an organization's security. This role goes far beyond technical assessment; it tests the readiness of people, processes, and technologies in concert. Red Teamers orchestrate long-term, campaign-style operations, using tactics such as social engineering, physical security bypass, and bespoke tool development to accomplish specific goals aligned with realistic attack scenarios.

Operating under strict operational security (OPSEC) and rules of engagement, Red Teamers measure their success not only by identifying weaknesses but also by catalyzing meaningful organizational improvements. They provide deeply analytical reports on detection, response, and strategic security gaps, facilitating both technical remediation and business-level learning.

Key Responsibilities:

- Emulate the specific tactics, techniques, and procedures (TTPs) of real-world threat actors.
- Conduct multi-week or multi-month campaigns that test people, process, and technology.
- Use advanced techniques, social engineering, physical security tests, and custom tool development.
- Report comprehensively on Blue Team detection, response, and strategic gaps.

Red Teamers take testing to a new level. Their objective-based assessments test not only for technical issues but also for the organization's ability to detect, respond to, and adapt to them. For example, a Red Team engagement might quietly gain access to sensitive data while remaining undetected, closely mirroring the methods of actual adversaries. Their value is measured not just in the discovery of flaws but also in triggering organizational growth and resilience.

A Week in the Life: From Scoping to Storytelling

So, what does this work actually look like? Let's follow Ramesh through a typical client engagement.

> **Monday**: Kick-Off & Scoping Ramesh starts not with hacking tools but with a video call. He finalizes the "Rules of Engagement", clarifying the client's systems, limits, timelines, and expectations. Professionalism and trust-building are paramount; success begins with listening and achieving a clear agreement.
>
> **Tuesday & Wednesday**: The Hunt Testing begins with reconnaissance, gathering information on web servers and applications, followed by probing with a mix of automated scanners and manual exploration. Ramesh looks for common flaws, SQL injection, XSS, and misconfigurations, documenting every step in secure logs. He collaborates with Blue Team contacts, sharing insights as needed and respecting boundaries.
>
> **Thursday**: The "Eureka!" After hours of meticulous work, Ramesh discovers a flaw in session handling that enables him to escalate privileges and access sensitive data. The thrill of discovery is immediately followed by thorough documentation: technical details, screenshots, and, crucially, an explanation of business risk.

Friday: The Report. Most of Friday isn't "hacking," but writing. Ramesh compiles a clear and actionable report that explains the risks to both technical staff and non-expert decision-makers. He meets with technical teams and company leadership to answer questions and build a roadmap for stronger defenses. His real value isn't just breaking in, but helping organizations mature and learn with practical guidance.

Global Perspectives and Collaborative Teams

Today's offensive security work is highly collaborative. Many organizations blend Red and Blue teams in "purple teaming," promoting shared learning and rapid business-wide resilience. Experts come from diverse backgrounds, including computer science, gaming, puzzle-solving, psychology, and communications. Whether you're a coder, a competitor, a communicator, or simply persistent, offensive security rewards diverse mindsets and deep curiosity.

A Red Team engagement at a major retailer, for example, led to the discovery of a critical flaw just days before it could be exploited on a large scale. The Red Team's creative approach, coupled with strong communication with Blue Team and GRC teams, helped avert a costly breach and drove important technological and strategic improvements.

Recruiter's Corner

"When I'm hiring for a junior pentester role, a degree and certifications are nice, but they don't tell me if you can do the work. Candidates with GitHub profiles showcasing their custom scripts, or a blog with detailed TryHackMe or Hack The Box write-ups, instantly move to the top. Practical portfolios demonstrate passion, curiosity, and the hands-on skills required by the job. But I also look for teamwork, adaptability, and the ability to explain findings to everyone, from engineers to executives."

The Certification Ladder: Your Ascent as a Tester

Certifications here are about practical performance, not theoretical memorization.

Step 1: Foundation, CompTIA Security+ establishes a baseline of knowledge on how systems are built, defended, and attacked. This is essential groundwork for both Red and Blue paths.

Step 2: Practical Lab, eJPT (eLearnSecurity Junior Penetration Tester). This beginner-friendly, highly practical exam uses a real lab environment. You conduct a real penetration test, applying the techniques you have learned to identify vulnerabilities.

Step 3: Industry Standard, OSCP (Offensive Security Certified Professional). The OSCP is the gold standard: a rigorous, 24-hour, hands-on exam. You break into multiple vulnerable machines on a simulated network, using all your skills and adaptability. It's a trial by fire, testing persistence, adaptability, and practical know-how. "Try Harder" is its defining mantra.

Career Spotlight: Meet Alex, the Penetration Tester

Alex's security journey began in online Capture The Flag competitions, challenging digital puzzles that ignited a passion for persistence and creative thinking. Their college years were filled with Hack The Box sessions, and every success was documented in a personal blog. This hands-on portfolio, not just a degree, landed Alex's internship.

"Preparing for the OSCP was the hardest thing I've ever done. It taught me to be meticulous, resilient, and never to quit after failure. After passing, recruiters responded instantly. My advice? Start doing. Try learning on platforms like TryHackMe, record your journey in a blog or GitHub repository, and document your process. Employers appreciate not just your wins, but also your obstacles and how you overcame them. Your passion and persistence are your best resume."

Action Station: My Offensive Path Action Plan

You've seen the roles, workflows, and the certification path. Now, take your first step with this checklist:

- **Choose a Learning Platform**: Create an account on a hands-on platform (TryHackMe, Hack The Box, PortSwigger Web Security Academy).
    - My Choice: ___________________________
- **Select a Foundational Skill**: Dedicate time to learning a new foundational skill (e.g., Python scripting, Linux basics, understanding web protocols).
    - My Skill Focus: ___________________________
- **Identify a Target Certification**: Set a long-term goal for a certification.
    - My Target Cert: ___________________________

- **Start Your Portfolio**: Create a place to document your learning journey (e.g., blog, GitHub repo, shared notes).
    - **My Portfolio: ____________________________**

Capture both your breakthroughs and setbacks. Offensive security is about learning from every challenge and proving your growth, curiosity, and resilience to future employers.

5 THE DEFENSIVE PATH: SECURITY OPERATIONS AND INCIDENT RESPONSE

If the offensive path is for those drawn to taking things apart, the defensive path is for those who find purpose in holding them together. This is the world of the Blue Team, the vigilant guardians who stand on the digital front lines, day and night, ensuring the systems that power our world remain safe, stable, and resilient.

Great defenders win not by passively reacting, but by being vigilant and smart: they think like attackers, anticipate new tactics, techniques, and procedures (TTPs), and design detection strategies that cut through even the most cunning forms of obfuscation. Modern defense is an active, continuous hunt —a high-stakes intellectual challenge requiring you to know your digital territory so intimately that you can spot anything or anyone that doesn't belong. You must blend preparedness, methodical investigation, and composure in high-pressure situations. For defenders, the mission is clear: protect and serve the organization every minute, every day, all year round.

The Roles of the Defensive Path

Let's look at the roles of the defensive path.

Security Operations Center (SOC) Analyst

Under the Blue Team, we discussed the role of the SOC Analyst. However, the **Roles of the Defensive Path: Security Operations Center (SOC) Analyst** and the **Blue Team: SOC Analyst** both describe the same core position. However, their descriptions offer different perspectives, emphasizing distinct facets of the SOC Analyst role. Below is a detailed comparison highlighting overlap and unique emphasis:

Aspect	Defensive Path Description	Blue Team Description
Conceptual Framing	Focuses on the analyst's *real-time situational awareness*, pattern recognition, and alert enrichment. Uses analogies (air-traffic controller).	Emphasizes operational role of *continuous monitoring* and *frontline defense*; direct, practical orientation.

Key Skills Highlighted	Pattern correlation (processes, command-line analysis); MITRE ATT&CK mapping; threat intelligence enrichment; "noise to signal" conversion; tuning SIEM for smarter alerts.	Real-time alert monitoring; incident triage/escalation; initial containment actions; reporting; SIEM and EDR/XDR maintenance; SOP and documentation management.
Responsibility Scope	Stresses the *analytical prowess* and ability to see broad patterns from isolated alerts, including refining alerts to reduce fatigue.	Details classic job duties: monitor, investigate, escalate, respond, report, optimize, and document.
Tools/Techniques	Specific mention of MITRE ATT&CK techniques, correlating parent/child processes, IOC enrichment from threat sources, and SIEM tuning.	Specifies SIEM, EDR/XDR, and real-time monitoring tech, plus playbook and SOP creation.
Depth of Role	Focus on mature analysts, alert tuning, contextualization, and improved team performance.	Emphasizes *24/7 monitoring*, structured incident response, procedural maintenance, and team communications.
Audience	Written for those interested in the depth, technique, and strategic thinking behind the role.	Written to define the foundational tasks and expectations for hiring, onboarding, or team alignment.

Defensive Path vs. Blue Team (SOC Analyst)

What's the Same?

- Monitoring and responding to security alerts/incidents.
- Triage, investigation, escalation, and initial response.
- Use of SIEM and EDR/XDR technologies.
- Analyst acts as a filter of noise, converting alerts into actionable intelligence.

- Continuous tool tuning and improvement.

What's Different?

- **Defensive Path:**
    - More narrative, "live operations" and mindset-driven, focus on how analysts interpret and enrich data, pivot from single alert to broad threat patterns, and improve detection capabilities.
    - Spotlight on analytical depth, threat intelligence enrichment, mapping techniques (MITRE ATT&CK), fatigue reduction, and evolving team practices.
- **Blue Team:**
    - More structured, task-based, and process-oriented, lists standard daily duties, reporting functions, playbook/SOP management, and classic incident lifecycle workflow.
    - Emphasis on procedural rigor, operational responsibilities, documentation, and reporting for management.

Incident Responder

An Incident Responder is a cybersecurity expert who leads the organization through technical and procedural crises, operating at the intersection of technology, business continuity, and cross-functional coordination. Their mission: to rapidly detect, contain, eradicate, and recover from cybersecurity incidents, while ensuring every action is fully documented, legally compliant, and strategically aligned.

Incident Responders develop formal incident response playbooks, conduct proactive drills to prepare teams, and coordinate with IT, legal, HR, and communications throughout the attack lifecycle. They analyze incidents thoroughly to pinpoint root causes, enabling continuous improvement in security readiness. Clear communication and precision timestamping of all actions are critical to preserving evidence and tracking decisions, whether during a real incident or in simulated exercises.

Key Responsibilities:

- Lead the technical, procedural, and cross-functional response to active cybersecurity incidents, from detection to containment, eradication, and recovery.
- Develop and maintain formal incident response (IR) playbooks, and run tabletop drills or "fire drills."
- Conduct thorough post-incident analysis to pinpoint root cause and recommend strategic improvements.
- Coordinate with IT for containment, with legal for evidence

preservation, with HR if insiders are involved, and with PR for consistent external messaging during a crisis.

- Ensure every technical and non-technical action is clearly timestamped and documented.
- Review logs, alerts, SIEMs, host, and network data for early signs of compromise.
- Assess severity, escalate incidents appropriately, and allocate resources.
- Identify precursor vulnerabilities, advise mitigation.
- Manage digital forensics (disk/memory imaging, artifact collection) to ensure evidence integrity.
- Advise management on notification obligations post-breach.
- Lead debriefs, update tools/processes, and foster improvement across teams.
- Collaborate with training and awareness teams to disseminate findings.

When a major incident is declared, the Incident Responder serves as the crisis manager and technical lead, navigating the organization through chaos. While the technical team isolates infected servers, the IR lead aligns with business continuity, legal, and communications teams to ensure that forensic evidence is preserved (chain of custody), strategic decisions are documented, and everyone is working from a unified playbook. In reality, and through exercises, they prepare the organization for swift, smooth reactions to the unexpected.

Digital Forensics Analyst

A Digital Forensics Analyst is a cyber-investigator who meticulously reconstructs the sequence and scope of digital incidents. They collect, preserve, and analyze digital evidence, such as files, logs, memory images, and network traces, in a defensible and repeatable manner, maintaining a strict chain of custody and abiding by legal standards. Their work supports both technical remediation and legal/criminal investigations, requiring precision, patience, and detective-level analytical skills.

Digital Forensics Analysts use specialized forensic toolsets (e.g., Volatility, KAPE, Velociraptor, timeline analysis) to recover deleted or hidden artifacts, reconstruct attacker actions, and detail how a breach or malicious act unfolded. They document their methodology and findings in reports tailored for engineers, executives, or courtroom use, ensuring their analysis withstands regulatory or legal scrutiny.

Key Responsibilities:

- Conduct deep investigations into compromised systems to understand the full scope and root cause of security incidents.
- Preserve, collect, and analyze digital evidence in a forensically sound

manner, maintaining a strict chain of custody (with hashing, e.g., MD5/SHA-256).

- Recover deleted or hidden files, reconstruct timelines, and attribute attacker actions using logs, endpoint protection, and network data.
- Prepare detailed, unbiased forensic reports for technical stakeholders, management, or legal/court proceedings.
- Use industry tools and workflows (e.g., Volatility for memory analysis, KAPE or Velociraptor for IR triage, timeline analysis for event reconstruction).
- Dissect malicious software to determine function and origin.
- Extend investigations to smartphones, cloud accounts, and SaaS data sources.
- Defend analysis in court or regulatory proceedings if necessary.
- Work closely with legal, law enforcement, IT, and incident response teams.
- Refine, document, and teach forensic procedures for business/agency readiness.
- Stay updated with evolving systems, anti-forensics, encryption, and data recovery challenges.

The Digital Forensics Analyst is the discipline's "detective," piecing together fragments of evidence to build a clear and verified narrative. Their rigor ensures organizational lessons, compliance, and, in severe cases, criminal charges are supported by facts, not assumptions.

Forensics is about patience, precision, and an analytical mind. A successful analyst can turn disparate technical data into a compelling story of "what really happened."

A Shift in the SOC: From Alert to Resolution

Let's step into the shoes of Anjali, a junior SOC Analyst, during a high-stress shift at a major financial company in Mumbai:

> **14:00**: The afternoon shift begins quietly. Anjali reviews dashboards of network traffic, SIEM alerts, and threat intelligence feeds. She closes out routine false positives (tuning rules as she goes), documents minor events, and checks system patch statuses. Here, discipline is everything: it's like monitoring a thousand cameras for that one out-of-place movement.
>
> **15:23**: An EDR (Endpoint Detection and Response) tool flags unusual PowerShell activity on a finance server, from an account that shouldn't need it. The commands are obfuscated, an early sign of malicious intent (MITRE ATT&CK T1059).

15:25: The hunt begins. Anjali acknowledges the alert and checks the server's logs for parent/child processes, network connections, and DNS requests. She correlates user behavior with recent administrative changes and runs the suspicious IP address against multiple threat intelligence feeds. MITRE ATT&CK techniques and the TTPs hint at something serious.

15:35: A quick intelligence check returns confirmation: the IP is linked to a known ransomware group's command-and-control infrastructure (e.g., T1071). Anjali pivots, searches for similar connections across the network, and documents her pivot path so that the next analyst can follow her logic.

15:37: Calm under pressure, Anjali calls the IR lead. She states: "I have a confirmed malicious C2 connection from our accounting server, matching the TTPs of the FIN-10 ransomware group. Recommend immediate containment."

15:40: Coordinated response begins. The Incident Response team isolates the server, initiates backup restoration, notifies legal to preserve volatile memory (via imaging/hashing), and alerts PR for internal messaging. While they battle the malware, Anjali continues hunting for related activity, broadening and deepening the search.

Her quick detection and composed escalation transform what could've been a major financial disaster into a contained event. The critical factor: vigilance, smart pivoting, and precise, actionable communication.

After the Storm: Purple Teaming and Lasting Lessons

After the incident is resolved, the defense continues. The organization conducts a Purple Team roundtable, a structured collaboration between Blue and Red Teamers, to turn lessons into lasting detections. New SIEM rules and YARA/Sigma signatures are developed from the attack's TTPs, playbooks are updated, and incident response and threat hunting exercises are rehearsed. This cycle turns yesterday's weaknesses into tomorrow's strengths.

Recruiter's Corner

"Technical skills are the price of admission, but not enough to stand out. I want to know how you handle pressure. Provide an example, technical or not, of how you faced a crisis and your step-by-step response. In security, panic is the enemy; the best defenders are those who think clearly when everyone else scrambles.

I also look for pattern recognition and prioritization. If you're triaging 50 alerts in an hour, what gets attention first and why? Show me your thought process. I want someone who can distinguish high-risk threats from mere noise and escalate smartly."

The Certification Ladder: Building Your Defensive Shield

For defenders, certifications validate your ability to analyze data, follow processes, and use detection and IR tools effectively.

Step 1: The Universal Foundation (CompTIA Security+):
Defenders need only essential knowledge in risk management, network architecture, and core security concepts.

Step 2: First Defensive Mission (CompTIA CySA+ or BTL1).

- CompTIA CySA+: Certifies analytical abilities, data correlation, and hands-on SOC/tactical defense skills.
- Blue Team Level 1 (BTL1): 100% practical. In a simulated live incident, you investigate, triage, and respond, showing real capability.

Step 3: The Incident Command Standard (GIAC GCIH).
A gold-standard, hands-on exam proving mastery in technical steps, process, and orchestration from detection to recovery.

Optional Next Steps:

- **Threat Hunting**: Blue Team Level Ops (BTLO) or enter SANS SEC555 territory for deeper hunts and adversary emulation.
- **Forensics**: GCFA or engage in DFIR (Digital Forensics/Incident Response) hands-on labs and competitions (e.g., Magnet CTFs).
- **Leadership**: Progress to incident manager or GRTP/managerial streams.

Action Station: My Defensive Path Action Plan

Build your own defensive strategy and skillset:

- **Choose a Home Lab Project**: Set up a practical project. (Examples: Security Onion VM; a Wazuh SIEM; learn Wireshark; practice log analysis with Zeek/Suricata).
    - My Project: ______________________________

  Starter lab idea: Windows VM + Linux VM + SIEM + Zeek + a safe malware sample (from a trusted source) for EDR/SIEM pivot drills.

- **Find a Go-To Resource**: Subscribe to a blog, threat feed, or podcast

(e.g., SANS Internet Storm Center, "The CyberWire," BleepingComputer).
  - My Resource: ____________________________

- **Identify a Target Certification**: Pick a path and set a long-term cert goal.
  - My Target Cert: ____________________________

- **Develop a Key Skill**: Choose a critical non-technical skill (e.g., crisis communication, meticulous notetaking, clear escalation processes, personal wellness under stress).
  - My Skill Focus: ____________________________

Defender's Resilience: The Learning Loop

Defense is a marathon, not a sprint. You can use after-action reviews (AARs) to refine your detection rules, automate repetitive tasks, and conserve your energy and well-being. Calm, rested defenders make the smartest and most creative decisions. Burnout helps the adversary, not the mission.

Success comes not just from the next tool or certification, but from a habit of learning, collaborating, and consistently improving, one alert, one investigation, and one after-action review at a time.

6 THE STRATEGIST'S PATH: RISK, COMPLIANCE, AND GOVERNANCE (GRC)

We have met the Guardians on the walls (the Blue Team) and the Testers who probe for weaknesses (the Red Team). But who decides which jewels in the kingdom demand the strongest defense? Who writes the laws that the soldiers must follow? And who negotiates the treaties to ensure peace and stability with the rest of the world? This is the crucial work of the "Royal Council", the domain of Governance, Risk, and Compliance (GRC).

GRC professionals translate legal, technical, and financial languages so leaders can choose the right risks to take and the wrong ones to avoid. Here, a background in law, business, or finance can be as valuable as a degree in computer science, and success is driven by clarity, consistency, and above all, integrity.

The Roles of the Strategist's Path

Let's look at the roles of the strategist's path.

Risk Analyst

A Risk Analyst is a forward-looking strategist who identifies, assesses, documents, and communicates the threats facing an organization's data, operations, finances, and reputation. Working closely with business, technical, and compliance leaders, they use recognized frameworks (such as NIST Cybersecurity Framework, ISO 27005, or FAIR) to methodically evaluate both the likelihood and impact of varied risk scenarios, including cyber attacks, insider threats, regulatory non-compliance, and third-party/vendor exposures.

The Risk Analyst maintains a detailed risk register, tracks ownership and remediation, and facilitates effective risk treatment decisions: acceptance, mitigation, transference, or avoidance. They produce regular reports that compare mitigation costs with estimated loss exposure and help decision-makers make informed, prioritized choices.

Key Responsibilities:

- Identify and assess potential risks to the organization's data, operations, and reputation.
- Use frameworks (NIST Cybersecurity Framework, ISO 27005, or FAIR for quantitative modeling) to analyze likelihood and impact.

- Maintain a formal risk register with fields for risk owner, likelihood, impact, treatment plan, and due date.
- Advise business and technical leaders on whether to accept, mitigate, transfer, or avoid risk, and review the register on a monthly/quarterly cadence.
- Evaluate third-party exposures before onboarding or renewal.
- Ensure all controls and risk treatments align with regulatory frameworks (GDPR, PCI-DSS, HIPAA, etc.).
- Assess security policies, controls, and operational practices to uncover gaps.
- Track emerging threats, industry trends, and business changes.
- Advise and support teams during incidents or near-misses, updating risk posture in real time.
- Educate stakeholders and promote a consistent risk-aware mindset across the organization.

Risk analysts are forward-thinking strategists who ensure the organization has a clear-eyed view of future obstacles. When feasible, they quantify scenarios using FAIR to estimate probable loss exposure and compare mitigation costs with acceptance costs.

A Week in the Life of a Risk Analyst

Let's follow Nidhi, a Risk Analyst at a fast-growing e-commerce company in Gurgaon:

> **Monday**: Kick off. The company is considering a new cloud-based HR platform. Nidhi leads the risk assessment, conducting interviews with HR, IT, and Legal to identify privacy constraints (GDPR/DPDP). She requests the vendor's SOC 2 Type II report, reviewing subservice organizations ("who else touches our data?") and any carve-outs.
>
> **Tuesday & Wednesday**: The Investigation. Nidhi scrutinizes the vendor's documentation and builds a data flow diagram. She reviews the company's business impact analysis (BIA) to quantify potential losses and align contractual Recovery Time Objectives (RTOs) and Recovery Point Objectives (RPOs) with the BIA's expectations.
>
> **Thursday**: Translating Risk Into Action. Nidhi synthesizes findings: the vendor's backup policy is vague. She decomposes a projected loss: "If ransomware takes out the system, we might lose all payroll data for a week, totaling an estimated □2 Crore impact based on productivity loss, overtime, IR retainer fees, and potential statutory penalties." She proposes requiring a stronger SLA clause.

Friday: The Committee. Nidhi presents to the security steering group. She provides a risk heat map and walks through accept/mitigate/transfer decisions. The execs demand SLA changes. Nidhi assigns a risk register entry with an owner, a treatment plan, and a due date, and tracks management's actions.

Compliance Analyst

Compliance Analyst was presented under **GRC (Governance, Risk, and Compliance)**. In contrast, the Strategist's Path may differ in framing, focus, and practical emphasis, even if the foundational responsibilities remain largely the same.

What Stays the Same

- **Core mission:** Ensuring the organization's compliance with laws, regulations, standards, and internal policies.
- **Key tasks:** Policy development, monitoring regulatory changes, training, audits, risk assessment, compliance reporting, and guidance.
- **Cross-functional collaboration:** Working with technical, legal, managerial, and operational teams to embed compliance into every aspect of the business.

Dimension	GRC Listing (Traditional/Operational)	Strategist's Path (Forward-looking/Advisory)
Focus	Day-to-day operations, monitoring, audit, and documented adherence	Shaping compliance strategy, anticipating changes/trends
Position	Enforcer and subject-matter expert in operations, policy, and controls	Advisor, risk communicator, partner in organizational change
Scope	Implementing controls, maintaining documentation, and passing audits	Designing company-wide roadmaps, championing best practices
Output	Reports, audit trails, incident support, compliance checks	Strategic analysis, executive presentations, scenario planning
Mindset	Compliance as a safeguard	Compliance as a competitive differentiator or enabler
Examples	Mapping technical controls to regulations, supporting incident response	Influencing M&A due diligence, geographic expansion, and innovation platforms

GRC vs. Strategist's Path (Compliance Analyst)

Where the Emphasis May Differ

Should the Responsibilities Change?

- **Definitions** will be nearly identical, but the **strategic path** emphasizes thought leadership, foresight, and change agency more heavily.
- **Key responsibilities:** Fundamental tasks (audit, policy, reporting) remain, but Strategy roles may de-emphasize some operational items (e.g., evidence collection, KPIs) in favor of risk forecasting, translating compliance trends for leadership, and integrating compliance with business growth or transformation projects.
- **Skillset:** A Strategist path often calls for advanced communication, forward-thinking, and influence, helping shape policy at the leadership table, not just enforce it.

Security Auditor

A Security Auditor is an independent evaluator responsible for assessing the design and operational effectiveness of an organization's security controls and compliance with industry/regulatory standards (such as ISO 27001, NIST, PCI-DSS, SOC 2, HIPAA, etc.). Security Auditors plan, execute, and report on systematic audits, using walkthroughs, sampling, technical tools, and re-performance testing to uncover control weaknesses, compliance gaps, and emerging risks. Their findings are documented and rated by severity, with remediation tracked to closure. Security Auditors serve as objective advisors, ensuring risk treatments are credible and controls truly work in practice, not just on paper.

Key Responsibilities:

- Plan and lead independent audits to evaluate security control effectiveness.
- Test control design and operating effectiveness via walkthroughs, sampling, and re-performance.
- Produce formal audit reports that rate findings by severity and assign remediation owners.
- Track remediation SLAs to closure and follow up on the implementation of findings and exceptions.
- Map security controls to business goals and regulatory frameworks: Ensure audits address both compliance and strategic risk priorities.
- Interview stakeholders and review policies/procedures: Assess control understanding and foster a security-first culture.
- Identify and recommend risk mitigation actions: Provide practical,

actionable improvement strategies for technical and business leaders.
- Review logs, change management, incident response, and business continuity plans: Confirm holistic organizational readiness.
- Monitor compliance with evolving standards and threats: Stay current on the latest regulations, cyber threats, and audit best practices.
- Document and preserve audit evidence for regulator/external review: Maintain clear audit trails for accountability.

Auditors are objective advisors, ensuring control design and actual operation are aligned, and that risk treatment is credible, not wishful.

The Governance Cadence & Key Processes

A Security Steering Committee meets monthly to review the risk heat map and exception aging, and to make formal accept/mitigate/transfer decisions. This creates a cycle of life: policies define intent; controls execute it; evidence proves it; audits test it; remediation continuously closes gaps.

The Control Owner is the specific individual accountable for the day-to-day operation and effectiveness of a security control (e.g., the Network Team Lead is the Control Owner for the Firewall Policy, while the Risk Manager is the Risk Owner for Network Risk). Mature GRC teams use GRC Automation Platforms, such as ServiceNow GRC or Archer, to streamline attestations, centralize evidence, and manage the full audit lifecycle.

Third-Party and Privacy in Practice

Vendors and data dominate today's risk surface. Strategists must:
- Tier vendors by data sensitivity and integration impact.
- Review SOC 2/ISO 27001 reports and penetration test summaries.
- Include right-to-audit clauses and breach notification timelines in Data Processing Agreements (DPAs).
- For privacy: maintain records of processing, perform Data Protection Impact Assessments (DPIAs), and assess cross-border data transfers.

Metrics That Matter

Modern GRC teams track and report meaningful measures such as:
- Time to close audit findings and remediate issues.
- Percentage of controls with current evidence and on-time attestations.
- Aging of risk exceptions and their compensating controls.
- Percentage of key vendors with current assurance.
- Training completion rates and simulated phishing fail rates.

Broader Career Pathways in the Strategist's Realm

Let's look at the career pathways in the Strategist's realm:

- Business Information Security Officer (BISO): Owns the risk posture for a specific business unit and aligns security strategy to its revenue objectives.
- Security Program Manager: Owns the GRC roadmap, orchestrates cross-functional work, and tracks progress against objectives and key results (OKRs).
- Privacy/Data Protection Officer (DPO): Drives lawful data handling, manages Data Subject Rights requests, and oversees privacy diligence.
- Third-Party Risk Lead: Owns the entire vendor risk management lifecycle, from onboarding and monitoring through to contract exit.

Career Spotlight: From Law Student to Risk Manager Rohan's journey started in law school. "I realized future legal challenges would be about data and tech." At a tech startup, his ability to translate regulations into practical steps made him invaluable. After earning his CRISC, he now leads a team. "My advice to non-technical people: embrace your translator skills, they're rare and needed."

Recruiter's Corner "For GRC, translation is your superpower. Can you explain 'unpatched server vulnerability' to a marketing VP as 'a flaw that could expose all our customer data'? Can you take a clause from a privacy law and help an app team build exactly what's required? GRC pros who can back up their advice with metrics are in high demand."

The Certification Ladder: Building Your Strategic Authority

Step 1: The Foundational Layer (CompTIA Security+)

Step 2: Practitioner's Credentials (CISA or CRISC)

- **CISA**: Validates audit, control, and assurance skills.
- **CRISC**: Premier risk management cert; shows you align risk with business strategy.

Step 3: Leadership Aspiration (CISM or CISSP)

- **CISM**: Focuses on governance and organizational leadership.
- **CISSP**: The gold standard for security leaders.

Action Station: My GRC Path Action Plan

- **Choose a Framework**: Familiarize yourself with a foundational GRC framework. (NIST CSF, ISO 27001, PCI-DSS).
    - My Choice: ____________________________

- **Highlight a Non-Technical Skill**: Identify a "translator" skill in your background (writing, project management, presentation).
    - My Skill Focus: ___________________________

- **Research an Industry**: Look up compliance regulations for a sector you care about (healthcare/HIPAA, banking/RBI).
    - My Industry Focus: ___________________________

- **Draft a Risk Register Entry**: From Nidhi's scenario, create an entry. Add a review date and approver.

- **Policy Mapping**: Take one policy (e.g., 'Data backups must be recoverable in 24h') and list two controls. Note the evidence source and attestation frequency for each control in your control mapping.

- **Set a Certification Goal**: Which GRC credential fits your path?
    - My Target Cert: ___________________________

Your GRC influence comes from clarity, consistency, and integrity. Say what matters, measure what counts, and follow through. Mature strategists don't just pass audits; they drive smarter business bets and build trust with colleagues. Done well, GRC enables smarter, faster, and safer decisions.

7 THE BUILDER'S PATH: SECURITY ENGINEERING AND ARCHITECTURE

We have met the vigilant Guardians who defend the castle walls and the strategic Royal Council that writes the laws. But who designs the castle itself? Who architects the secret passages, reinforces the gates, and builds the watchtowers in a way that makes the entire structure inherently strong? This is the vital work of the Builders.

The Builder's Path is for those who believe security shouldn't be an afterthought, a layer of paint applied at the end of a project. Instead, they see it as the foundation. Their mission is to "shift left," moving security from the end of the development process to the very beginning. When security engineering is done right, teams move faster and with more confidence, and innovation thrives —not stalls.

The modern security engineer is a catalyst for speed. They utilize automation, code, and clever design to create "paved roads", secure pathways that enable developers to build and deploy software faster and more securely than ever before. This is the path for those who love to create, solve complex design puzzles, and build the resilient systems of the future.

The Roles of the Builder's Path

Let's look at the roles of the builder's path.

Security Engineer

A Security Engineer is responsible for designing, implementing, and managing an organization's security infrastructure, ensuring data, networks, and systems are safeguarded against cyber threats. Working cross-functionally, Security Engineers build and maintain protective technologies, such as firewalls, identity and access management systems, and endpoint protection, and are pivotal in developing security standards, conducting vulnerability assessments, automating remediation, and driving organization-wide awareness of secure configurations.

Modern Security Engineers leverage advanced tools (e.g., SIEMs, EDR, privilege management, network segmentation) and scripting languages (e.g., Python, Bash, PowerShell) to automate monitoring, patch management, and incident response. They collaborate with IT, development, and infrastructure teams, serving as subject matter experts to align business initiatives with robust security practices.

Key Responsibilities:

- Design, implement, and manage core security infrastructure (firewalls, identity and access management systems, endpoint protection).
- Develop security standards and hardening guidelines for servers, networks, and operating systems.
- Conduct vulnerability assessments and help manage the enterprise-wide patch management lifecycle.
- Serve as the security subject matter expert for IT, infrastructure, and application development projects.
- Analyze activity, respond to threats/incidents, tune detection, and alerting.
- Participate in incident response efforts: Investigate breaches, collaborate in containment, and recovery.
- Implement controls for standards (ISO, PCI-DSS, HIPAA, GDPR) and assist in audits.
- Use scripting and orchestration tools to streamline monitoring, reporting, patching, and remediation.
- Train IT/development staff, produce documentation, and promote secure practices across teams.
- Evaluate current defenses, research threats/trends, recommend/implement new solutions.

As a Security Engineer, you'll work with tools like SIEM, EDR (Endpoint Detection and Response), privilege management systems, network segmentation (VLANs), and certificate management, using automation scripting (Python/Bash/PowerShell) to scale your work.

Cloud Security Engineer

A Cloud Security Engineer designs, implements, and manages the security of cloud environments, such as AWS, Microsoft Azure, or Google Cloud Platform (GCP), to ensure data confidentiality, integrity, and availability. This professional configures cloud-native security tools (e.g., GuardDuty, Azure Sentinel, IAM, and key management), automates the deployment and validation of security controls using Infrastructure as Code (IaC) practices (e.g., Terraform or AWS CDK), and continuously assesses configurations to ensure compliance with requirements.

Cloud Security Engineers proactively monitor for threats, lead cloud security incident response, and integrate best-practice controls into DevOps workflows.

They master tools including Identity and Access Management (IAM), cloud-native security monitoring and event tools, KMS (Key Management Service), CSPM (Cloud Security Posture Management), and scripting to automate audits, detection, and remediation.

Key Responsibilities:

- Design and implement secure cloud architectures in environments like AWS, Microsoft Azure, or Google Cloud Platform (GCP).
- Manage and configure cloud-native security tools (e.g., AWS GuardDuty, Azure Sentinel, IAM policies).
- Automate the deployment and static analysis (e.g., Terraform code scans) and dynamic validation (e.g., post-deployment configuration reviews) of security controls using Infrastructure as Code (IaC).
- Conduct security reviews of cloud services and ensure configurations meet compliance requirements.
- Continuously monitor cloud environments, investigate alerts, and lead cloud-based incident response.
- Create and maintain cloud security policies and SOPs for secure deployment and usage.
- Ensure and document compliance with standards like SOC 2, PCI-DSS, HIPAA, or ISO 27001 in the cloud.
- Partner with architecture, DevOps, and engineering teams to shift security left and educate on cloud security best practices.
- Scan for vulnerabilities, remediate issues, and advise on securing cloud workloads.
- Address security for Kubernetes, Docker, and other modern cloud technologies.

As a Cloud Security Engineer, you will master IAM (Identity and Access Management), cloud-native security monitoring, cloud KMS (Key Management Service), CSPM (Cloud Security Posture Management) tools, and write infrastructure-as-code in languages like Terraform or AWS CDK.

DevSecOps Engineer

A DevSecOps Engineer embeds security throughout every phase of the software development lifecycle by integrating automated security checks into CI/CD pipelines, championing secure development practices, and building a culture where security is a shared, automated responsibility. This role requires expertise with automation stacks (GitHub Actions, GitLab CI/CD, Jenkins, Azure DevOps), container security (Docker, Kubernetes), cloud and infrastructure security controls, and vulnerability management, acting as a bridge between development, operations, security, and GRC.

DevSecOps Engineers implement Policy as Code (PaC) to codify compliance and governance rules directly into deployment and infrastructure automation, ensuring that security and regulatory mandates are automatically and uniformly enforced in highly scalable environments.
Key Responsibilities:

- Integrate automated security testing tools into the CI/CD (Continuous Integration/Continuous Deployment) pipeline.
- Secure containerized application environments (using technologies like Docker and Kubernetes).
- Work directly with developers to identify and remediate vulnerabilities found in their code.
- Champion a security-first culture within fast-paced DevOps and software engineering teams.

A Day in the Life of a DevSecOps Engineer

Let's follow Rahul, a DevSecOps Engineer at a fintech startup in Bengaluru, to see the Builder's mindset in action.

10:00 AM: The Pipeline Review. Rahul's day starts not with an alert, but with a notification: a developer's code has failed a build. The automated security scanner he integrated has detected a critical vulnerability in a new library, automatically blocking the insecure code from reaching production.

10:15 AM: Collaboration, Not Conflict. Rahul opens a Slack channel with the developer, explains the vulnerability, links to a report on the flaw, and points them to a safer, pre-approved version of the library. He's not a gatekeeper; he's a guide.

2:00 PM: Building a New Guardrail. To prevent this problem from happening again, Rahul writes a new policy-as-code using Terraform. This code will automatically enforce a rule that prevents the use of any software library with known critical vulnerabilities in all future projects.

4:30 PM: A Lasting Fix. He submits his new code. Once approved, it's deployed in minutes. The security control he just designed is now automated and enforced across the entire organization. Modern builders like Rahul protect not only the company's future, but its velocity, customer trust, and shared reputation.

A Builder's Impact: Teaching and Collaboration

Builders work across silos. They collaborate with Development, IT, product, and business teams to ensure security is part of every discussion. The most effective builders often teach by example, designing reference architectures that entire organizations adopt. Leading or co-facilitating a threat modeling exercise (e.g., STRIDE, DREAD, or attack trees) is one of the most valuable leadership and risk-spotting skills you can offer, showcasing both technical depth and a collaborative spirit. Furthermore, reviewing peers' Terraform, pipeline, or automation scripts and providing clear, constructive feedback is itself a builder's power skill.

The most advanced builders use Policy as Code (PaC) with tools such as the Open Policy Agent (OPA) or its cloud-native equivalents. PaC allows GRC rules (e.g., "All data must be encrypted") to be translated directly into code that automatically enforces compliance across all environments, making Rahul's work immediately scalable and auditable.

Metrics That Matter

The impact of a Builder is measurable. They track metrics that connect their work to real-world risk reduction, such as:

- Mean time to patch critical vulnerabilities.
- Number of high-risk misconfigurations caught early in cloud posture scans.
- Percentage adoption of secure-by-default templates by development teams.
- Pipeline build fail rates due to security gates, indicating that automated controls are working.

Recruiter's Corner

"Don't just tell me you know AWS. Tell me about a time when you used AWS security services to secure an S3 bucket in a personal project. Show me a GitHub repository with a Terraform script you wrote. In the cloud world, practical, hands-on project experience —even from a home lab —is infinitely more valuable than just a certificate. We hire builders who can prove they know how to build."

The Certification Ladder: Building Your Technical Credentials

Step 1: The Foundational Duo (Security+ and Cloud Provider Certs)

Step 2: The Cloud Security Specialist (AWS Security - Specialty or Azure AZ-500)

Step 3: The Architectural Standard (CCSP)

Beyond the Core Roles: Specialization and Community Impact

Security Sales Engineer (Pre-Sales Consultant): This is a highly valued path for security professionals with strong communication skills. They act as the deep technical bridge between the sales team and the customer, designing and demonstrating security solutions (products or services). This role uniquely requires a blend of Tester/Builder depth with the Strategist's communication and persuasion skills to thrive on client engagement and technical storytelling.

The Builder's path offers many branches for specialization. You can specialize as a Security Architect, Platform Security Lead, Application Security Lead, or Security Automation Engineer, and pursue advanced certifications for your target platform (e.g., AWS Certified Security, Specialty, Azure Security Engineer Associate AZ-500, or GCP Professional Cloud Security Engineer).
Furthermore, the most effective builders multiply their impact. Contributing your scripts, documentation, or policies to open-source projects or to internal company libraries (also known as inner sourcing) demonstrates both advanced skills and leadership.

Career Spotlight: Meet Priya, the Cloud Security Engineer. Priya started her career as a software developer but was always drawn to the security implications of her code. "I started spending my free time in my own AWS account, learning how to use services like IAM to lock down my personal projects." She documented everything on a blog. When a Cloud Security Engineer role opened up, her practical portfolio was the deciding factor. "My advice is simple: be curious and build things. The cloud gives you a free lab to experiment in. That practical experience is what will set you apart."

Action Station: My Builder's Path Action Plan

- **Choose a Cloud Platform**: Create a free-tier account on a major cloud platform (AWS, Azure, GCP).
    - My Choice: ______________________________

- **Learn a Security-by-Design Principle**: Read about and understand one core principle (The Principle of Least Privilege, Defense in Depth).
    - My Principle Focus: ______________________________

- **Start a Hands-On Project**: Start a small, practical project in your cloud lab (Create a secure S3 bucket, build a web server and configure its security group, write a small Terraform script).
    - My First Project: ______________________________

- **Document Your Project**: Document your project with a screenshot, a README file, or a blog post; clarity and visibility matter as much as code.

- **Track your own results**: How quickly can you identify and fix a misconfiguration? Can you automate remediation? Use these lab metrics to demonstrate improvement in interviews or portfolios.

- **Identify a Target Certification**: Set a long-term goal for a Builder-focused certification.
    - My Target Cert: ___________________________

Builders who teach, automate, and document their solutions multiply their impact and help organizations stay secure by default.

8 BEYOND THE KEYBOARD: BUILDING YOUR PERSONAL BRAND AND INFLUENCE

Imagine two candidates interviewing for a junior security analyst role. Both have similar degrees and hold the same foundational certifications. Their technical skills, on paper, appear to be identical. One candidate answers questions competently. The other tells a compelling story about how a CTF competition ignited their passion, explains technical concepts using clear analogies, and asks insightful questions that show they've thought deeply about the company's challenges.

Who gets the job?

The answer is almost always the second candidate. In a field crowded with technical talent, the skills that set you apart are rarely about what you know; they are about how you communicate what you know, how you connect with others, and the professional reputation you build. Technical skills get you the interview. The skills we discuss in this chapter get you the job, the promotion, and the ability to make a genuine impact.

This chapter is about building your X-factor. It's about crafting your professional brand, developing your persuasion skills, and honing the emotional intelligence that turns a technician into a leader.

Crafting Your Professional Brand: You Are More Than Your Resume

A brand isn't just a logo; it's your professional reputation. It's the story people tell about you when you're not in the room. A strong personal brand answers three questions: Who are you? What do you stand for? And what value do you bring?

Your Professional Story

Your brand starts with your story. What is your "origin story" in technology and security? What unique path brought you here? Whether you arrived via self-study, a bootcamp, or switched from another career, your unique perspective is an asset; authenticity matters more than fitting a stereotype. A genuine story is memorable and makes you relatable.

Your Digital Storefronts: LinkedIn & GitHub

LinkedIn: Your Professional Portfolio. Treat your LinkedIn profile not as a static resume, but as a dynamic professional landing page. A living profile is an active one. Share wins and learning moments, but don't be afraid to post about failed projects and what they taught you. Authenticity builds trust. A key part of building your brand is also amplifying others. Endorsing classmates or colleagues for their skills and sharing useful content from others ("signal boosting") raises your visibility and builds your reputation as a collaborator.

GitHub: Your Proof of Work. GitHub is the definitive portfolio for demonstrating practical skills. You can use it to host your notes from platforms like TryHackMe, share simple automation scripts, and document your projects. This provides concrete proof of your curiosity and hands-on ability.

Quantify Your Brand

When you write your story in your LinkedIn summary or describe a project on GitHub, include tangible proof. Add numbers or specific artifacts whenever possible. For example, instead of "Worked on a project," try: "Launched four security automation scripts used by classmates," or "Wrote a blog post on cloud security that has over 2,000 views." A growth mindset shines when you also mention what didn't go as planned, what you learned, and how you adapted.

Influence Without Authority: The Art of Persuasion

Influence isn't just how many people you know, but how many seek your advice, share your posts, or recommend you to others. Pay attention to which projects or posts start conversations or are referenced by others; this real-world engagement is the best validation. Early in your career, you won't have formal authority, so your success will depend on your ability to persuade.
Framing Your Accomplishments with STAR

To tell a powerful story about your work, use the STAR method. It's a simple framework to structure your accomplishments for interviews, resumes, and performance reviews.

- **Situation**: Briefly set the scene and context.
- **Task**: Describe your responsibility or the goal.
- **Action**: Explain the specific steps you took.
- **Result**: Share the outcome, quantifying it whenever possible. Writing down 2-3 of your key projects in the STAR format is one of the best ways to prepare for any interview.

Emotional Intelligence (EQ): Your Secret Weapon

Emotional Intelligence (EQ) is the ability to understand and manage your own emotions, and to recognize and influence the emotions of others. In a technical field, high EQ is a rare and powerful advantage.

Empathy and Active Listening

When an employee clicks a phishing link, the low-EQ response is blame. The high-EQ response is empathy: "Thank you for reporting this. These attacks are getting very clever. Let's walk through what happened." This approach builds a culture of trust. You can actively build these communication skills. Join Toastmasters, take a short public speaking course, or present at a local security meetup, even a small one. These activities build clarity and confidence under pressure.

Becoming a Security Advocate: From Jargon to Clarity

Every security professional is also a teacher. They continually educate colleagues, managers, and stakeholders about digital risks. Embracing this role is fundamental to scaling your impact.

This advocacy extends beyond the office. The best advocates also educate their peers, family, and community. Consider running a short "security basics" workshop for non-tech-savvy friends or helping a local community group with safe password practices and phishing awareness. This not only helps others but also sharpens your own ability to explain complex topics and builds your confidence. The more generously you share, the more your brand and network will grow organically.

Finally, remember to make brand maintenance a habit. Update your profiles every quarter with new projects, learnings, or events to keep your story fresh and up to date.

Action Station: The LinkedIn Profile Makeover

Use this checklist to transform your LinkedIn profile from a student resume into a professional brand statement.

- **Professional Photo**: A clear, high-quality headshot.
- **Aspirational Headline**: Go beyond "Student." Include what you do and what you're passionate about.
- **Compelling "About" Summary**: Tell your story, mention 2-3 key

skills (with proof points!), and state your goals.
- **Featured Section**: Link to your GitHub, a blog post, or a project you're proud of.
- **Experience & Projects**: Detail your projects using the STAR method to describe the outcome.

Action Station: Crafting Your 30-Second Elevator Pitch

You have 30 seconds to introduce yourself to a hiring manager. Use this formula:

1. **Who You Are**: "Hi, I'm [Your Name], and I'm a [Your Role/Aspiration]."
2. **What You're Passionate About**: "I've always been fascinated by [Your Topic], and I've spent the last year building my skills in..."
3. **What Value You Bring**: "...practical labs and even built a [Your Project]."
4. **What You Want**: "I'm a huge admirer of [Company's] work, and I'm looking for opportunities to bring my skills to a team like yours."

Once you've drafted your pitch, practice it aloud, record yourself, or get feedback from a peer. Consider adapting a shorter version for your social media profile bios.

9 THE LAUNCH SEQUENCE: NAILING THE INTERVIEW AND LANDING THE ROLE

You've explored the paths and started building your skills. Now comes the final act of translation: converting your potential, projects, and passion into a compelling package that convinces a hiring manager you are the right person for their team. The job application process, from your resume to the final offer, is the launch sequence for your career.
This chapter is your tactical, behind-the-scenes guide to acing every stage, turning anxiety into confidence.

The Resume That Gets Noticed: Your Digital Handshake

Your resume has about ten seconds to make an impression. It's a marketing document designed to achieve one goal: to get you the interview.
Start with a Powerful Summary. At the very top, add a one or two-sentence summary that states your focus and quantifies your value.

Example: "Security student with 200+ hours hands-on SOC labs (Wazuh/Wireshark), 10+ pentest write-ups, and OSINT CTF finalist experience; built policy-as-code checks in GitHub Actions. Seeking SOC Analyst roles."

Adopt a Project-First, ATS-Friendly Format. Place a "Hands-On Projects" section at the top. Use a simple, single-column format, keep verbs in the past tense (unless the project is ongoing), and avoid tables or graphics. For early-career candidates, limit your application to one page.

Tailor Your Resume to the Job Description. Don't send the same resume to every place. Mirror 6–10 keywords from the job posting, but keep the context honest (e.g., "Built Sigma rules in Wazuh SIEM for DNS exfil alerts"). Under each project, add a "Tech Stack" line listing the tools you used and a location/time context (e.g., "Home Lab, 2024"). To reduce link sprawl, consider creating a single portfolio hub page (on GitHub Pages or Notion) and linking to that in your resume header.

The Power of Your Network: Internships and Connections

Internships: The Ultimate Audition. An internship is a three-month-long interview. Actively seek them out, and once you're in, be a sponge: take notes, ask questions, and offer to help with any task.

Networking with Purpose Networking is about building genuine connections. After a chat, send a 3-sentence thank-you note, include one sentence on how you used their advice, and ask if you can keep them posted to sustain the relationship.

Example: "Hi [Name], thanks again for your time last week. I tested your advice on exploring cloud security posture tools and set up a lab with Wiz. I'd love to keep you posted, appreciate your guidance." The fastest route to warm introductions is to join and volunteer at local meetups, such as OWASP, BSides, or Null.

The Interviewer's Lens: What They're Really Looking For

The interview is designed to uncover what your resume can't convey.
Core Traits They Seek:

1. **Curiosity and Passion**: Demonstrate this by asking thoughtful questions.
2. **A Methodical Problem-Solving Process**: Talk through your thought process out loud. When you don't know an answer, use a structured approach: "I don't recall the exact command, but I'd start by checking the logs, then I'd validate the process connections, and if that failed, I'd pivot to analyzing network traffic."
3. **Coachability and Humility**: Arrogance is a red flag. It's okay to admit you don't know something. Even better, frame a small failure to show resilience: "I first tried to solve it with approach X (here's why), but it failed because of Y (here's what I learned). I then pivoted to approach Z, which was successful."

Preparation Drills: Turning Anxiety into Confidence

- **Practice Aloud**: Conduct at least two mock interviews with a friend or mentor. Record yourself to check for clarity and filler words.
- **Create a Mini Runbook**: Before any interview, have a short document ready with 3 STAR stories, five technical topics you can explain, and five thoughtful questions to ask them. For virtual interviews, keep this one-page crib sheet printed out and in view on your camera.

Insider's Take: An Interview Horror Story (And How to Avoid It). We once interviewed a candidate who was technically brilliant but arrogant. He constantly interrupted us and tried to bluff when he was unsure of something. We didn't hire him. A brilliant jerk can destroy a team's culture. We'll take a humble and curious candidate over a technical genius with a bad attitude every time."

Recruiter's Corner "My biggest pet peeve? When a candidate says, 'No, I don't have any questions for you.' It's an instant red flag that shows a complete lack of curiosity. A passionate candidate will always have questions."

The Art of Storytelling: Using STAR in Your Interview

When an interviewer asks, "Tell me about a time when...," they are seeking a specific story. Use the STAR method. A quick tip: Keep the Situation/Task to ≈20% of your answer and the Action/Result to ≈80%; they want to know what you did and what happened.

Your Question Bank: What to Ask Them

Have 3-5 thoughtful questions ready. Mix them across these categories:

- **Team & Work**: "What will be my first meaningful project in the first 90 days?"
- **Learning & Growth**: "How do junior team members get mentorship and feedback here?"
- **Process & Culture**: "How do you run post-incident reviews or blameless retrospectives?"
- **Impact**: "What metrics matter most for success in this role?"

Handling Offers and Compensation

If you receive an offer, you can negotiate.

- **Evaluate the Total Package**: Look beyond the base salary. Ask about the on-call rotation, expected hours, remote/hybrid policy, tooling budget, and promotion/leveling frameworks.
- **Negotiate Thoughtfully**: Always express enthusiasm first. If you counter, anchor your request to market data and the value you've demonstrated. If the base salary is fixed, consider requesting a more generous learning budget, certification vouchers, or conference travel expenses.

Example: "I'm very excited about this offer. Based on market data and my demonstrated projects in cloud automation, could we explore a base salary in a specific range, or perhaps an increased learning budget for my upcoming AWS certification?

Action Station: Your Interview Playbook

- Create a 3-line resume summary that mirrors your target job description.

- Draft 5 tailored project bullets with metrics and a "Tech Stack" line.
- Create a "portfolio hub" link (e.g., on GitHub Pages) to organize your projects, screenshots, and write-ups in one place.
- Write five thoughtful questions you'll ask in your next interview, practicing them aloud.
- Create a 1-page interview crib sheet with your summary, 3 STAR bullets with metrics, and your top 5 questions.
- Conduct one technical and one behavioral mock interview with a peer; record and review it.
- Prepare a negotiation script that expresses enthusiasm, cites your value, and asks thoughtfully.
- Prepare your STAR stories:
    - **Story 1**: A Time I Solved a Problem
    - **Story 2**: A Time I Worked on a Team
    - **Story 3**: A Time I Failed or Made a Mistake

10 THE LONG GAME: FROM LEARNING TO LEADING

Congratulations. You have explored the paths, learned the strategies for breaking in, and equipped yourself with a map to begin your journey. Landing your first role in cybersecurity is a monumental achievement, a moment to be celebrated. But it is not the finish line.

It is the starting line.

The career you are about to embark on is not a sprint; it is a long and rewarding marathon. The knowledge and skills that get you your first job are merely the foundation. The true craft of a security professional lies in what you build upon that foundation over the years. This final chapter is about that long game. It's about cultivating the mindsets and strategies that separate a practitioner with a job from a leader with a lasting career.

Thriving on Change: The Learning Agility Mindset

There is one certainty in our field: the technology, threats, and tactics of today will be legacy in five years. The single most valuable skill you will ever possess is not mastery of a specific tool, but the ability to learn, unlearn, and relearn at a rapid pace. This is learning agility.

Cultivating this mindset is an active process:

- **Stay Insatiably Curious**: Dedicate a few hours each week to unstructured learning. The best professionals are always a little uncomfortable; they seek out new tools and topics, even those outside their comfort zone.
- **Embrace "Just-in-Time" Learning**: Get comfortable with not knowing everything but having confidence in your ability to find the answer quickly.
- **Look to the Horizon**: Pay attention to the emerging frontiers, from the role of AI in security to the long-term threat of quantum computing. A commitment to lifelong learning is the key to staying relevant.

The Power of Your Network: Your Personal Board of Directors

As your career progresses, you will find that the most complex problems are rarely solved alone. A support network is your personal "board of directors": a group of mentors, peers, and mentees who will challenge, support, and guide you.

- **Finding Mentors**: Be respectful of their time and specific in your asks: "I'm struggling to understand the path from analyst to architect. Do you have 20 minutes to share your experience?"
- **The Power of Peers**: Your peers are your most valuable, long-term resource. Nurture these relationships.
- **Becoming a Mentor**: The fastest way to solidify your own knowledge is to teach it to someone else. The cyber community thrives on service. When you share what you've learned, you build trust, raise your visibility, and give others a hand up.

From Practitioner to Thought Leader: Crafting Your Security Vision

To transition into a leader, you must move from just executing tasks to developing your own perspective. You must find your voice and your vision.

- **Develop a Specialization**: After gaining broad experience, choose one or two areas to go deep in. This specialization is the foundation of your unique value.
- **Share Your Vision**: You don't have to be a master to start sharing; in fact, the act of teaching is one of the fastest ways to learn. Write tutorials about what you're currently studying, record short videos explaining a new concept, or help a peer who is one step behind you. As you grow, you can present at meetups, contribute to open-source projects, and establish yourself as a producer of insight.

Career Trajectories: From Analyst to the Boardroom

A career in this field is rarely a straight line. Sometimes, the best next step is a lateral move into an adjacent function, such as privacy, audit, or sales engineering, or even a brief pause to upskill. Every path is valid. As you progress, your growth will be measured not just by promotions, but by your expanded responsibilities, the people you mentor, your public contributions, or the systems you've fundamentally improved.

After your foundational years, your career can branch into two primary directions:

1. **The Specialist Path (Individual Contributor)**: For those who love the deep, hands-on work, growing to become a Principal Security Architect or a world-renowned expert in a niche field.
2. **The Leadership Path (Manager)**: For those who find satisfaction in building teams and scaling their impact through others, on a journey

from Senior Analyst to CISO.

Career Spotlight: The CISO Journey

Priya, the CISO of a major retail company, started as a junior analyst. The turning point came when she began asking why incidents were happening, not just how to close the tickets. This led her to a role in risk, where she learned the language of business. "The first time I had to explain a vulnerability to our Head of Sales was terrifying," she recalls. "I had to talk about risk to customer relationships and revenue." Excelling at this "translation," she eventually became a manager. Today, as a CISO, her days are filled with budget planning and strategy development. "My job now," she says, "is to build the best team and tell a clear story about security that empowers the business. The technical skills got me in the door, but the communication and leadership skills are what got me to this seat."

Action Station: My 5-Year Plan

Use this prompt to sketch out the first leg of your long-term career journey. As you do, document your real-world impact, projects, people, and moments where you made a difference, not just where you advanced in your job title.

1. My 5-Year Vision:

- Where do I see myself in five years? (Specialist or Leadership path?)
    - ____

2. Key Skills to Acquire:

- What are 2-3 technical skills I will need? (e.g., Advanced cloud security, Python).
    - ____

- What are 2-3 "beyond the keyboard" skills I need to develop? (e.g., Public speaking, project management).
    - ____

3. My "Personal Board of Directors":

- Who is one person senior to me whose career I admire and could learn from?
    - ____

- Who is one peer I can collaborate with and learn alongside?
    - ____

4. My First Step:

- What is one concrete action I can take this month to start moving toward my 5-year goal?
  - ____

- Schedule a calendar reminder to revisit this plan each year, reflect on what changed, and celebrate unexpected wins. As you do, update your professional story on LinkedIn and in your portfolio to reflect your new goals and accomplishments.

The Journey is the Reward

You have reached the end of this guide, but you are at the very beginning of your real adventure. A career in information security is a commitment to a lifetime of learning and growth. Cybersecurity can be high-pressure, and sustainable careers require rest, healthy boundaries, and well-being practices. Burnout is an industry risk.

It's normal to experience detours and even failures, missed promotions, tough incidents, or certifications that take more than one try. These moments don't define you; they shape your character and persistence. A career is not a straight line but a series of pivots, lessons, and restarts.

Your impact will be measured not just by the roles you hold, but by the people you help, the ideas you share, and the resilience you develop. The journey truly is the reward.

APPENDIX A: THE GLOBAL CYBER MARKET: A GUIDE TO INTERNATIONAL JOB HUBS

One of the most exciting aspects of a career in cybersecurity is that your skills are highly portable globally. A talented SOC analyst in Mumbai has the same foundational knowledge as one in London or Toronto. As you advance in your career, you may consider opportunities to work abroad to gain diverse experience, learn from different business cultures, and tackle unique challenges.

This guide provides a high-level overview of some of the world's most prominent cybersecurity hubs. Keep in mind that every international move involves significant research into visa requirements, cost of living, and cultural integration.

North America

1. Washington D.C. Metropolitan Area, USA (The "DMV")

- **Why It's a Hub**: The epicenter of the US federal government and defense-related cybersecurity, home to government agencies, military cyber commands, and the world's largest defense contractors.
- **Key Strengths**: Government & Defense Contracting, Threat Intelligence, Public Policy.
- **Considerations**: Many roles require US citizenship and security clearances, a significant barrier for foreign nationals.

2. Silicon Valley / Bay Area, California, USA

- **Why It's a Hub**: The global heart of the tech industry, home to Big Tech and a massive ecosystem of venture-backed cybersecurity startups.
- **Key Strengths**: Startup Ecosystem, Product Security, Cloud Security, Research & Development (R&D).
- **Considerations**: Extremely high cost of living and fierce talent competition.

3. Dublin, Ireland

- **Why It's a Hub**: The "Silicon Valley of Europe," hosting the European headquarters for many major US tech companies. A critical center for data privacy and governance within the EU.
- **Key Strengths**: Data Privacy & Governance (GDPR), Cloud Security, Trust & Safety.

- **Considerations**: Many EU-based jobs require practical acquaintance with GDPR, and occasionally proficiency in other European languages. The housing market is very competitive.

Europe & The Middle East

1. London, United Kingdom

- **Why It's a Hub**: A leading global financial center with massive demand for cybersecurity in banking and FinTech.
- **Key Strengths**: Financial Services Security, FinTech, GRC, Penetration Testing.
- **Considerations**: Financial services clients often prize UK-specific experience and knowledge of FCA/PRA regulations. Post-Brexit visa rules should be researched thoroughly.

2. Tel Aviv, Israel

- **Why It's a Hub**: A global cybersecurity powerhouse, often called "Silicon Wadi," fueled by a deep talent pool and a world-leading number of security startups.
- **Key Strengths**: Offensive Security, Threat Research, Startup Culture, R&D.
- **Considerations**: The market is highly advanced and prizes deep technical expertise, often found in candidates with backgrounds in CTFs, bug bounties, or elite military cybersecurity units.

3. Dubai, UAE

- **Why It's a Hub**: A rapidly growing business hub with a strong focus on smart city initiatives, finance, and securing major international events.
- **Key Strengths**: Smart City/IoT Security, Financial Services, GRC.
- **Considerations**: A fast-paced, multicultural environment that is a major consumer and implementer of security technologies.

Asia-Pacific (APAC)

1. Singapore

- **Why It's a Hub**: The premier business, financial, and technology hub of Southeast Asia, with heavy government investment in technology and security.
- **Key Strengths**: Financial Services, Government Security, and Regional Threat Intelligence.
- **Considerations**: A highly competitive market with a high cost of living. Local certifications or knowledge of MAS (Monetary Authority

of Singapore) guidelines are highly valued in the banking sector.

2. Sydney & Canberra, Australia

- **Why It's a Hub**: A mature and growing market, split between the government and defense sectors in the capital, Canberra, and the financial/technology sectors in Sydney.
- **Key Strengths**: Government Security (Canberra), Financial Services (Sydney), Cloud Security.
- **Considerations**: Holding or being eligible for Australian government security clearances can unlock many additional roles, especially in Canberra. Visa processes are well-defined but can be lengthy.

Final Considerations for a Global Career

Your Global Job Search Strategy

- **Use global and specialized job boards**: Platforms like LinkedIn, Indeed, and Glassdoor, as well as industry-specific sites like InfoSec Jobs, are excellent for searching by country or for companies known to sponsor international candidates. Use LinkedIn's filters to search for roles that offer visa sponsorship.
- **Research local compensation**: Before applying, research the current salary bands in your target locations on sites like Glassdoor and Levels. Fyi, or by speaking with local recruiters.
- **Network at international events**: Attending major conferences, such as Black Hat, DEF CON, and RSA, or regional ones like NullCon (in India), can be a fantastic way to meet international recruiters and hiring managers.

Navigating the Move

- **Visas are the Biggest Hurdle**: Securing a work visa is the most complex part of the process. Always start your research on the official government immigration websites of your target country.
- **Credentials Travel Well, but Local Knowledge Matters**: Certifications such as CISSP, CISM, AWS Security, and OSCP are universally respected. However, be prepared to upskill in local regulations (such as data protection laws) to become a more competitive candidate.
- **Language and Culture are Accelerators**: Even when roles are advertised in English, the ability to speak the local language or understand local business etiquette can accelerate your advancement and build client trust, especially in leadership roles.
- **Explore "Borderless" Career Paths**: The rise of remote work has created new opportunities. You don't always need to relocate to work for an international company. Consider "digital nomad visas" or roles

in fully distributed teams that hire the best talent, regardless of location.
- **Build Your Career at Home First**: The easiest path to an international role is often to build a strong foundation of experience in your home country. Many professionals are transferred internationally after proving their value to a multinational company.

Your Pre-Application Checklist

Before you begin applying for roles abroad, confirm the following:
1. Work visa and sponsorship requirements for your target country.
2. Local salary expectations and how they compare to the cost of living.
3. Needed or preferred local certifications or regulatory knowledge.
4. Language skills that may be required or beneficial.
5. Connect with a few professionals on LinkedIn in that city to ask for firsthand advice.

APPENDIX B: THRIVING IN A REMOTE-FIRST WORLD: TIPS FOR REMOTE WORK SUCCESS

The global shift towards remote and hybrid work has fundamentally changed the technology landscape. For a field as inherently digital as cybersecurity, this has been a natural evolution, opening up a global talent pool for companies and unprecedented opportunities for professionals.

However, remote work is more than just a perk; it's a distinct way of working that requires a specific set of skills and a high degree of personal discipline. Excelling in a remote role requires you to be just as intentional about your communication and visibility as you are about your technical work. This guide provides a playbook for finding and succeeding in a remote-first career.

1. Finding Your Remote Opportunity

The demand for remote cybersecurity talent is immense. Here's how to position yourself for success.

- **Where to Look**:
  - **Standard Job Boards**: Platforms like LinkedIn, Indeed, and Naukri now have powerful "Remote" or "Work from Home" filters. Use them as your primary search tool.
  - **Remote-First Job Boards**: Websites like We Work Remotely, Remote.co, and FlexJobs are dedicated exclusively to remote positions, often featuring companies with strong remote cultures.
  - **Target Remote-First Companies**: Many modern tech and security companies are "fully distributed" by design (e.g., GitLab, Automattic). Researching and targeting these companies can be a great strategy, as their entire culture is built around remote collaboration.
- **Standing Out as a Remote Candidate**: Since the hiring manager can't meet you in person, your digital presence is your first impression. A remote-first hiring process emphasizes written communication, since the team primarily functions that way. Your application, resume, and emails are your first audition. They must be clear, professional, and meticulously proofread to demonstrate your ability to communicate effectively in a remote setting.

2. The Core Skills for Remote Success

Working effectively from a distance requires cultivating specific habits.

Proactive and Asynchronous Communication

In an office, you can rely on spontaneous conversations. Remotely, communication must be more deliberate. The key is mastering asynchronous communication, communicating with full context so that your colleagues can respond at their own convenience, often across different time zones.

- **Provide Full Context**: Never make someone ask for more information. A poorly written message, such as "Hey, the server is down," can create stress and require multiple follow-ups. A well-written message provides a clear path to a solution:

"Hi team, I'm unable to reach the production web server at [IP address] since 10:15 AM IST. I'm getting a 'Connection Timed Out' error and have confirmed it's not my local network. Can anyone else in the APAC region confirm? Here's a screenshot of my error."

- **Document Everything by Default**: Your work, your processes, and your decisions should be documented in a shared, accessible place (like a team wiki, Confluence, or Notion page). This reduces repetitive questions, makes your work visible, and creates a searchable knowledge base that is invaluable for the entire team.
- **Over-Communicate Your Status**: This isn't about micromanagement; it's about building trust. A brief end-of-day summary in your team's channel ("Today I completed the firewall rule review. Tomorrow I will start scripting the automation. I am not blocked.") makes your progress visible and reassures your manager and teammates that work is moving forward.

Self-Discipline and Time Management

Your Home is Full of Distractions. Thriving remotely requires creating a structure for yourself.

- **Create a Dedicated Workspace**: Having a specific desk or room for work is crucial. This physical separation creates a powerful psychological boundary. "Entering" your workspace in the morning helps you focus, and "leaving" it at the end of the day helps you disconnect.
- **Set and Communicate Your Work Hours**: Define your start and end times and communicate them to your team, especially if you work across time zones. This helps manage expectations and protects your

personal time. When your workday is over, log off, close your laptop, and take a step back.

- **Block Your Time for Deep Work**: Your calendar is your most important tool. Block out 2-3 hour chunks of "deep work" time for tasks that require intense focus, like log analysis or policy writing. This protects you from "meeting fatigue" and ensures you have the uninterrupted time needed for high-quality technical work.

Building Trust and Visibility

Out of sight cannot mean out of mind. You must be intentional about building your reputation and fostering connections within your team.

- **Be Unfailingly Reliable**: Your reputation for dependability is your most valuable asset. Deliver high-quality work on time. Crucially, if you think you might miss a deadline, communicate it early, not at the last minute. Proactive honesty builds immense trust.
- **Be a Visible Team Player**: Don't be a ghost who only appears to submit work. Be an active, helpful presence on your team's communication channels. Ask insightful questions, offer to help a colleague who is stuck, and share interesting articles or threat reports. Your positive digital presence will be noticed.
- **Schedule Human Connection**: Recreate the "water cooler" conversation. Schedule regular, informal 15-minute 1-on-1 video calls with your teammates and manager with no agenda other than to connect, chat about the weekend, or discuss a hobby. These moments build the human bonds essential to effective teamwork.

Mastering Your Remote Security Posture

As a security professional, you are a role model and a prime target. Your home network is now an extension of the corporate network.

- **Secure Your Home Network**: Go beyond the basics. Change the default admin password on your Wi-Fi router, use strong WPA2/WPA3 encryption, and keep its firmware up to date. For extra security, create a separate "Guest" network for your personal and smart-home (IoT) devices to keep them isolated from your work computer.
- **Be Hyper-Vigilant About Phishing**: Attackers know that remote workers are more vulnerable because they can't quickly turn to a colleague and ask, "Hey, does this email look legitimate?" Scrutinize every unexpected email, especially those that create a sense of urgency or ask for your credentials.
- **Adhere to All Company Policies, Always**: It can be tempting to bypass the company VPN for a "quicker" connection, but doing so

exposes you and the company to significant risk. Follow all data-handling, device-management, and access-control policies without exception.

3. The Challenges to Prepare For

- **Isolation and Loneliness**: The lack of spontaneous social interaction is a real challenge. Be proactive about joining virtual team lunches or coffee chats. Outside of work, consider joining local professional meetups, a co-working space once a week, or online communities related to your hobbies to maintain a sense of connection.
- **The "Always On" Culture and Burnout**: When your office is always a few steps away, it's easy to fall into the trap of working late or checking messages at all hours. Protect your personal time aggressively. Turn off work notifications on your phone after your workday is done and communicate your boundaries clearly.
- **Career Progression**: It can sometimes feel harder to get noticed for promotions when you're not physically in an office. This is why keeping a "brag document," a running list of your accomplishments, projects, and positive feedback, is crucial. Proactively schedule regular career conversations with your manager to discuss your goals and share your ambitions.

APPENDIX C: A SPOTLIGHT ON DIVERSITY, EQUITY, AND INCLUSION (DEI) IN CYBER

For decades, the world of technology and cybersecurity has been working to overcome a persistent challenge: a lack of diversity. But in recent years, a powerful truth has become clear: Diversity, Equity, and Inclusion are not just social goals or "nice-to-haves." They are a strategic imperative for effective security.

An adversary can come from any background and have any motivation. They will exploit our biases and blind spots. If the teams defending our digital world are composed of people who all look, think, and were educated in the same way, they will inevitably share the same blind spots. While representation is improving, it's also important to acknowledge that structural and unconscious biases persist. Allies and leaders alike have a responsibility to recognize and actively address these challenges head-on. Building a team with a rich diversity of thought, experience, culture, and identity is one of the most powerful defenses an organization can have.

The “Why”: How DEI Strengthens Cybersecurity

It's not just a theory; research from institutions like Harvard consistently shows that diverse teams make better, faster decisions and outperform homogeneous teams, especially when tackling complex, novel problems such as those in cybersecurity.

- **Stronger Problem-Solving**: Diverse teams bring a wider range of perspectives and analytical approaches to a problem, leading to more creative and robust solutions.
- **Reduced Groupthink**: Homogeneous teams are susceptible to "groupthink," where assumptions go unchallenged. Diverse teams are more likely to question the status quo and spot hidden risks.
- **Reflecting the World We Protect**: A security team that reflects our globally diverse population is better equipped to understand and protect all communities.
- **Closing the Talent Gap**: Diversity also includes age, life experience, people re-entering the workforce, and career changers. There is no single, ‘correct’ path into cyber. Actively recruiting from this wider talent pool is the only sustainable way to fill the millions of open jobs.

Key Communities and Advocacy Groups

Finding a community of peers can be one of the most powerful accelerators for your career. It's important to remember that many people hold multiple identities (e.g., race, gender, neurodivergence); true inclusion values the richness of everyone's intersecting backgrounds and experiences. The following organizations offer mentorship, networking, and resources.
(Note: This is not an exhaustive list, but a great starting point.)

For Women in Security:

- **Women in CyberSecurity (WiCyS)**: A global organization with local chapters, an annual conference, a job board, and mentorship programs.
- **The Diana Initiative**: An annual conference and community focused on supporting women in InfoSec.

For Black Professionals in Security:

- **Blacks In Cybersecurity (BIC)**: A rapidly growing organization focused on creating a pipeline of Black talent through networking, mentorship, and its annual conference.
- **International Consortium of Minority Cybersecurity Professionals (ICMCP)**: A non-profit dedicated to the success of minority cybersecurity students and professionals.

For Hispanic & Latinx/a/e Professionals in Security:

- **Latinas in Cyber (LAIC)**: An organization dedicated to empowering Latinas in the cybersecurity industry.
- **Cyber Latinos**: A community focused on increasing the representation of Latinos in the field.

For LGBTQ+ Professionals in Security:

- **Out in Tech**: A global non-profit that unites the LGBTQ+ tech community, with a large and active membership of security professionals.

Global & Regional Initiatives:

- Many international and regional groups are making a huge impact. Consider global programs such as (ISC)²'s DEI initiatives and regional groups, including SheLeadsTech (globally), European Women in Security (EWiS), and Women in Cybersecurity Middle East (WiCSME).

Beyond Joining: How to Get Involved

- Seek out scholarships and grants specifically for underrepresented groups to attend major conferences like Black Hat, RSA, or DEF

CON.
- Participate in workshops on public speaking or submitting a "Call for Papers" (CFP) to help you get your voice heard at events.
- Join virtual panels, hackathons, and conference "villages" that are focused on creating safe and inclusive spaces for learning.
- Ask about "allyship" events or volunteer to be part of a local DEI task force at a conference or within your company.

How to Be an Effective Ally

If you are a member of a majority group, you play a critical role.
- **Listen and Amplify**: Actively listen to the experiences of your colleagues from underrepresented groups and amplify their voices and ideas.
- **Mentor and Sponsor**: Mentoring is giving advice. Sponsoring is using your influence to actively advocate for someone's career.
- **Challenge Bias**: If you hear non-inclusive language, challenge it respectfully. A simple, "What do you mean by that?" can be a powerful way to interrupt bias.
- **Join as an Ally**: All the communities listed above welcome and need allies. Your support makes a difference.

The future of cybersecurity is, by necessity, inclusive. Finding a community that supports you and being an active supporter of others are among the most important things you can do to build a long, successful, and fulfilling career.

Three Steps You Can Take Today

Building a more inclusive industry can feel like a massive task, but it starts with small, consistent, and intentional actions. Here are three meaningful steps you can take right now to contribute.

1. Follow and Actively Listen. Begin by actively listening to the conversations already happening in the community. Choose one of the DEI-focused organizations mentioned in this appendix, like WiCyS, Blacks In Cybersecurity, or a regional group, and follow their official page on LinkedIn or another social media platform. This isn't just about adding a name to your feed; it's about connecting with the leaders, challenges, and successes within that community. Pay attention to the issues they discuss, the leaders they celebrate, and the opportunities they share. This simple act of listening is the first and most important step in becoming a more informed and effective member of the security community.

2. Amplify the Work of Your Peers One of the most powerful things you can do to foster an inclusive environment is to use your own platform, no matter how small, to amplify the voices of others. Make it a habit to seek out exceptional work from your peers, especially those from backgrounds different from your own. This could be a well-written blog post, a clever solution in a lab, or an insightful comment in a class forum. When you find it, share it. Post a link on LinkedIn with a positive, specific comment like, "My classmate Priya just wrote a fantastic analysis of the latest cloud vulnerability. It's a great read!" This simple act gives them visibility, validates their work, and builds your own reputation as a supportive and collaborative professional.

3. Intentionally Invite Someone. Diverse teams don't happen by accident; they are built intentionally, one person at a time. The next time you are forming a study group, starting a Capture The Flag (CTF) team, or working on a new lab project, be mindful of who is in the room. Consciously extend an invitation to someone from a background that is less represented in the field, or simply someone you don't normally work with. This is not about tokenism; it's about recognizing that different perspectives make the team stronger. The person you invite will bring a unique perspective that could be the key to solving a problem your group would otherwise miss. This is how you start building the powerful, diverse teams the industry desperately needs.

APPENDIX D: THE ULTIMATE RESOURCE LIST: CURATED BLOGS, PODCASTS, AND CONFERENCES

Your learning journey doesn't end with this book. In fact, it's just beginning. The most successful professionals in cybersecurity are dedicated, lifelong learners. This appendix serves as your curated guide to news sources, blogs, podcasts, and communities to help you stay informed, connected, and up to date.

1. News, Blogs, and Newsletters (Written Content)

For Daily News & General Awareness

- **The Hacker News**: One of the most popular sources for breaking news on vulnerabilities and cyberattacks.
- **BleepingComputer**: An outstanding resource for detailed, easy-to-understand write-ups on new ransomware strains and malware campaigns.
- **Dark Reading**: A comprehensive news site with a great mix of breaking news, opinion pieces, and analysis of corporate security challenges.

For Deep Dives and Investigative Journalism

- Krebs on Security: Written by veteran investigative journalist Brian Krebs, this blog features deep dives into the world of cybercrime.
- Troy Hunt's Blog: An exceptionally clear blog on web security and data breaches from the creator of "Have I Been Pwned."
- SANS Internet Storm Center (ISC): A "daily diary" of the state of the Internet, run by a global community of security practitioners.

Seeking Out Diverse Voices

- A richer understanding of cybersecurity comes from listening to a wider range of experts. Actively seek out security perspectives from people with different backgrounds, geographies, and identities. Blogs and platforms like Dominique West's "Security in Color" and Tanya Janca's "We Hack Purple" community enrich your learning journey.

2. Podcasts (Auditory Learning)

For Daily and Weekly News Briefings

- **The CyberWire Daily**: A crisp, professional, and vendor-neutral daily briefing of all the top cybersecurity news.

- **Risky Business ("Risky.Biz")**: A weekly, in-depth news and analysis show, widely considered one of the best in the industry.

For Storytelling and Deep Dives

- **Darknet Diaries**: A masterfully produced podcast that tells the true stories of hacking, data breaches, and cybercrime.
- **Security Now**: A long-running, deep technical dive into the week's security news.

For Career Growth & Leadership

- **CISO Series Podcast**: Features a variety of shows focused on the real-world challenges and conversations happening at the leadership level in security.
- **Humans of InfoSec**: A podcast by Caroline Wong that shares the human stories and diverse career paths of people in the industry.

3. Real-Time News and Community Platforms

For the very latest breaking news, threat intelligence, and career advice, many professionals turn to real-time social platforms.

- **"InfoSec Twitter" (X) and Mastodon**: Follow respected security researchers, journalists, and community leaders on these platforms. It's often the fastest way to learn about a new vulnerability or gauge industry sentiment.
- **Discord and Slack Communities**: Many security groups, from the TryHackMe community to specialized channels for threat intelligence, operate on these platforms. They are excellent for asking questions, getting real-time help, and networking with peers.
- **Other Essential Platforms**: Communities like Reddit's r/netsec provide a constant stream of news and discussion, while sites like InfoSecWriteups on Medium are fantastic for reading tutorials and post-mortem analyses from other practitioners.

4. Conferences and Community Events

Conferences are about community, networking, and hands-on learning. Many now offer virtual editions or post their content in online libraries after the event. Major International Conferences

- **Black Hat, DEF CON, and RSA Conference**: These are the "big three" global conferences, primarily held in the USA, each with a different focus (corporate, hacker community, and business/vendor, respectively).
- **Notable Regional Conferences**: The global scene is vibrant. Look into respected events in Europe (e.g., BruCON, Troopers) and the

Asia-Pacific region (e.g., HITB Singapore, AusCERT) to get a worldwide perspective.

Key Indian & Regional Events

- **Nullcon**: India's premier international security conference, held annually in Goa. A must-attend event for professionals in the region.
- **BSides**: Community-organized, low-cost security conferences held in cities all over the world, including many in India (e.g., BSides Delhi, BSides Ahmedabad). They are the best place to start networking locally.
- **OWASP Local Chapters**: The Open Web Application Security Project has local chapters in most major cities that host regular, free meetups.

How to Use These Resources Effectively: Your Action Plan

Don't just passively consume, actively engage. Here's a simple plan to get started:

1. Subscribe to one core newsletter and commit to reading it weekly.
2. Listen to one podcast episode per week during your commute or while working out.
3. Join one local or virtual security meetup (like BSides or OWASP) this quarter.
4. Share your favorite finding from an article or podcast on your LinkedIn each month with your own one-sentence take.
5. Add new sources to your rotation as you discover them and your interests evolve.

As you progress, curate your own favorite sources, update your personal list regularly, and share them with others, becoming both a learner and a signal booster.

APPENDIX E: THE GLOSSARY OF KEY TERMS

AppSec (Application Security): The practice of finding, fixing, and preventing security vulnerabilities within software applications, including web and mobile apps.

Authentication: The process of verifying you are who you say you are. Think of it like showing your ID card to a guard. Passwords, fingerprints, and security tokens are all methods of authentication.

BIA (Business Impact Analysis): A process used in GRC to determine the potential effects of an interruption to critical business operations as a result of a disaster, accident, or emergency.

Black Hat: A major, highly technical, and professionally focused cybersecurity conference held annually in locations around the world, known for its cutting-edge research presentations.

Blue Team: The defenders. In the castle analogy, this is the team of Guardians responsible for protecting an organization's systems from cyberattacks.

BSides: A community-organized series of cybersecurity conferences held in cities all over the world, known for being more accessible and informal than major corporate conferences.

C2 (Command and Control): A server controlled by an attacker that is used to send commands to compromised systems (bots) and receive stolen data from them.

CCSP (Certified Cloud Security Professional): A high-level, vendor-neutral certification that validates expertise in cloud security architecture, design, operations, and compliance.

CI/CD Pipeline (Continuous Integration/Continuous Deployment): An automated workflow that helps software developers build, test, and release code quickly and reliably. DevSecOps integrates security scanning and testing directly into this "digital assembly line."

CISA (Certified Information Systems Auditor): A globally recognized certification for professionals who audit, control, and monitor an organization's information technology and business systems.

CISM (Certified Information Security Manager): A management-focused certification for professionals who design, build, and manage an enterprise's information security program.

CISSP (Certified Information Systems Security Professional): A high-level, advanced certification for experienced security practitioners that validates comprehensive knowledge across a wide range of security domains. Often considered a gold standard for security leadership.

Cloud Security: The sub-field of cybersecurity focused on protecting data, applications, and infrastructure hosted in a cloud environment (like AWS, Azure, or GCP).

Compliance: The "C" in GRC. The process of ensuring an organization adheres to specific rules or standards established by laws (such as the GDPR) or industry bodies (like PCI-DSS).

CRISC (Certified in Risk and Information Systems Control): A certification for professionals focused on enterprise IT risk management, validating their ability to identify and manage risk in alignment with business goals.

Critical Infrastructure: The physical and virtual systems and assets so vital to a society that their incapacity or destruction would have a debilitating impact, such as power grids, water supplies, and financial systems.

CSPM (Cloud Security Posture Management): A category of security tools designed to identify and remediate misconfigurations and compliance risks in cloud environments.

CTF (Capture The Flag): A popular type of cybersecurity competition where participants or teams solve security-related puzzles and technical challenges to find hidden digital "flags."

Cyberattack: A deliberate and malicious attempt to breach the information system of an individual or organization. Examples include DDoS attacks, ransomware, and data breaches.

Cybersecurity: The practice of protecting systems, networks, and data from digital attacks. Its goal is to maintain the confidentiality, integrity, and availability of information.

CySA+ (CompTIA Cybersecurity Analyst): An intermediate-level certification that focuses on the analytical skills used to detect and combat cybersecurity threats.

Data Breach: An incident where sensitive, protected, or confidential data is accessed, disclosed, or stolen by an unauthorized person.

DAST (Dynamic Application Security Testing): A type of security testing that analyzes an application from the "outside-in" while it is running, by simulating external attacks to find vulnerabilities.

DDoS (Distributed Denial-of-Service): An attack that aims to make a website or online service unavailable by overwhelming it with a flood of traffic from many different sources.

DEF CON: One of the world's oldest and largest "hacker" conferences, held annually in Las Vegas, known for its community-driven atmosphere and hands-on competitions.

DevSecOps: A cultural philosophy that integrates security practices ("Sec") into the DevOps (Development and Operations) process, making security a shared, automated responsibility.

DFD (Data Flow Diagram): A graphical representation of the flow of data through a system, used in GRC and security architecture to map out where sensitive data is and how it is protected.

Digital Forensics: The practice of collecting, preserving, and analyzing digital evidence from a security breach to reconstruct the attacker's actions.

Docker: A platform for building, shipping, and running applications in isolated environments called "containers."

DPIA (Data Protection Impact Assessment): A process used in GRC to help identify and minimize the data protection risks of a new project.

EDR (Endpoint Detection and Response): A cybersecurity solution that continuously monitors endpoint devices (like laptops and servers) to detect and respond to advanced threats that evade traditional antivirus software.

Elevator Pitch: A short, persuasive speech that you can use to introduce yourself, your skills, and your goals in the time it would take to ride an elevator.
Encryption: The process of scrambling data into a secret code so it can only be read by someone with the correct "key."

FAIR (Factor Analysis of Information Risk): A framework used in GRC for understanding, analyzing, and quantifying information risk in financial terms. Firewall: A network security device that monitors and controls incoming and outgoing network traffic based on a defined set of security rules.

GCIH (GIAC Certified Incident Handler): A certification that validates the skills required to manage and respond to active security incidents.

GDPR (General Data Protection Regulation): A comprehensive data protection and privacy regulation in the European Union that affects any organization worldwide that processes the data of EU citizens.

Governance: The "G" in GRC. The process of creating the formal policies, standards, and procedures that direct an organization's security efforts.

GRC (Governance, Risk, and Compliance): The strategic pillar of cybersecurity focused on setting policies (Governance), managing threats (Risk), and ensuring rules are followed (Compliance).

HIPAA (Health Insurance Portability and Accountability Act): A US federal law that requires the creation of national standards to protect sensitive patient health information.

IaC (Infrastructure as Code): The practice of managing and provisioning computer infrastructure through machine-readable code files, rather than through manual configuration.

IAM (Identity and Access Management): The security discipline that ensures the right people have the right level of access to the right resources, at the right time.

Incident Response (IR): The organized approach to addressing and managing the aftermath of a security breach or cyberattack, from containment to eradication and recovery.

(ISC)²: A global non-profit organization that specializes in information security training and certifications, including the highly respected CISSP.

ISO 27001: An international standard for managing information security. Organizations can be formally audited and certified against this standard to prove their security posture.

Kubernetes: An open-source platform for automating the deployment, scaling, and management of containerized applications like those built with Docker.

Malware: Short for "malicious software." A general term for any software designed to cause harm. Viruses, worms, spyware, and ransomware are all types of malware.

NASSCOM: India's premier trade body and chamber of commerce for the Tech industry in India.

NIST (National Institute of Standards and Technology): A US government agency that develops cybersecurity standards, guidelines, and best practices, such as the widely-adopted NIST Cybersecurity Framework (CSF).

Offensive Security: The practice of proactively finding security flaws by thinking and acting like an attacker. It is the domain of the Red Team.

OSCP (Offensive Security Certified Professional): A highly respected, hands-on certification for penetration testers that requires passing a grueling 24-hour practical exam.

OWASP (The Open Web Application Security Project): A global non-profit foundation focused on improving the security of software. They are famous for the "OWASP Top 10" list of critical web application security risks.

PCI-DSS (Payment Card Industry Data Security Standard): A set of security standards designed to ensure that all companies that accept, process, store, or transmit credit card information maintain a secure environment.

Penetration Testing (Pentest): An authorized, simulated cyberattack against a computer system, performed to evaluate its security. Also known as ethical hacking.

Phishing: A type of social engineering attack where an attacker sends a fraudulent message (typically an email) designed to trick a person into revealing sensitive information.

Playbook (Incident Response): A set of predefined, step-by-step instructions for responding to a specific type of security incident, such as a ransomware attack or data breach.

Policy: A formal set of rules and principles that guides an organization's decisions and actions.

Ransomware: A type of malware that encrypts a victim's files, making them inaccessible, and then demands a ransom payment to restore access.

Red Team: The attackers. A team that mimics the tactics of real-world adversaries to test an organization's defenses and the readiness of the Blue Team.

Resilience (Cyber Resilience): The ability of an organization to continue operating despite experiencing a cyberattack or security failure.

Risk: The potential for loss or damage when a threat exploits a vulnerability, often calculated as a combination of likelihood and impact.

Risk Register: A tool used in GRC to track and manage identified risks. It typically lists each risk, its likelihood, impact, owner, and mitigation plan.

RPO (Recovery Point Objective): The maximum acceptable amount of time during which data might be lost from a service due to a major incident. It answers the question, "How much data can we afford to lose?"

RTO (Recovery Time Objective): The target time within which a business process must be restored after a disaster or disruption to avoid unacceptable consequences. It answers the question, "How quickly must we be back up and running?"

SAST (Static Application Security Testing): A type of security testing that analyzes an application's source code from the "inside-out" to find vulnerabilities before the code is run.

SCA (Software Composition Analysis): A type of security tool that scans an application's code to identify all open-source components and any known vulnerabilities within them. Modern SCA also leverages to provide a full inventory for supply chain security and compliance.

Security by Design: A philosophy that aims to make systems as free of vulnerabilities as possible by building security in from the very beginning of the design process.

Shift Left: A practice in DevSecOps that involves moving security testing and consideration to the earliest possible point (i.e., to the "left") in the development lifecycle.

SIEM (Security Information and Event Management): A powerful tool used by SOC Analysts that collects and analyzes log data from across an organization's network to spot signs of a potential cyberattack.

SOC (Security Operations Center): A centralized team or facility responsible for continuously monitoring and defending an organization's security posture.

SOC 2 Report: An audit report that validates a service organization's security, availability, processing integrity, confidentiality, and privacy controls.

Social Engineering: The art of psychologically manipulating people into performing actions or divulging confidential information.

SQL Injection (SQLi): A common web application attack where an attacker inserts malicious SQL code into an input field to manipulate or steal data from the backend database.

STAR Method: A technique for answering behavioral interview questions by structuring an answer into four parts: Situation, Task, Action, and Result.

Terraform: A popular Infrastructure as Code (IaC) software tool that allows users to define and provision infrastructure using a declarative configuration language.

Threat: Any potential danger that could harm a computer system or organization. An attacker, malware, or a natural disaster can all be threats.

TTPs (Tactics, Techniques, and Procedures): The patterns of behavior and methods used by a specific threat actor or group to conduct cyberattacks.

Vulnerability: A weakness or flaw in a system's design, implementation, or operation that could be exploited by a threat to cause harm.

XSS (Cross-Site Scripting): A type of web application vulnerability where an attacker injects malicious scripts into content that is then delivered to other users' browsers, often to steal session cookies or other sensitive information.

Zero-Day: A vulnerability that is known to attackers but is not yet known to the software vendor or the public, meaning no patch is available.

APPENDIX F: QUICK-REFERENCE GUIDE TO ROLES AND CERTIFICATIONS

This appendix serves as a quick reference guide to many common roles and popular certifications in the cybersecurity industry. The certifications listed here are common recommendations and not exhaustive requirements. The field is constantly evolving, and the value of a specific certification can vary by country, industry, and employer.

Always use this guide as a starting point. The best way to determine which certifications are most valuable for you is to research job descriptions for the roles you are most interested in and see which credentials appear most frequently.

Defensive & Operations Path (The Blue Team)

Job Role	**Common & Recommended Certifications**
Information Security Analyst	• CompTIA Security+ • Certified Ethical Hacker (CEH) • GIAC Security Essentials (GSEC) • Certified Information Systems Auditor (CISA)
Network Security Engineer	• GSEC • CISSP • Certified Network Defender (CND) • Cisco Certified Network Associate (CCNA) Security
Incident Response Analyst	• GIAC Certified Forensic Analyst (GCFA) • GIAC Certified Incident Handler (GCIH) • EC-Council Certified Incident Handler (ECIH)
Security Operations Center	• GCIH • CompTIA Security+

(SOC) Analyst	• CompTIA Cybersecurity Analyst (CySA+)
Forensic Analyst	• GCFA • EnCase Certified Examiner (EnCE) • Computer Hacking Forensic Investigator (CHFI)
Threat Intelligence Analyst	• CEH • GIAC Cyber Threat Intelligence (GCTI) • Certified Threat Intelligence Analyst (CTIA)

Offensive Path (The Red Team)

Job Role	Common & Recommended Certifications
Ethical Hacker / Penetration Tester	• CEH • GIAC Penetration Tester (GPEN) • Offensive Security Certified Professional (OSCP)

Strategy & Governance Path (The GRC Team)

Job Role	Common & Recommended Certifications
Cybersecurity Auditor	• Certified Internal Auditor (CIA) • Certified Information Systems Auditor (CISA) • Certified in Risk and Information Systems Control (CRISC)
Compliance Officer	• CISA • CRISC • Certified Information Privacy Professional (CIPP)
Security Awareness & Training Specialist	• Certified Security Awareness Professional (CSAP) • Certified Professional in Learning and Performance (CPLP)

Engineering & Architecture Path (The Builders)

Job Role	Common & Recommended Certifications
Security Architect	• CISSP • Certified Cloud Security Professional (CCSP) • Certified Information Security Manager (CISM)
Security Engineer	• CISSP • CISM • CCNP Security

Leadership & Specialized Roles

Job Role	Common & Recommended Certifications
Security Consultant	• CEH • CISSP • CISM • OSCP
Security Operations Manager	• CISM • CISSP • Project Management Professional (PMP)
Cryptographer	• CISSP • Certified Secure Software Lifecycle Professional (CSSLP)

ABOUT THE AUTHOR

Ashish Chugh is a technologist, educator, and creative thinker with over three decades of experience spanning audio/video editing, IT infrastructure, cybersecurity, software development, and digital learning. Known for his ability to translate complex technical concepts into accessible insights, Ashish has authored and reviewed hundreds of certification exams, technical courses, study guides, and instructor-led training programs across emerging technologies, including cloud computing, AI, blockchain, and cybersecurity.

His work bridges the worlds of innovation and education, including national-level skill development frameworks and curricula for large corporations. Ashish's passion lies in empowering non-technical audiences to engage confidently with technology, fostering a culture of lifelong learning.

Ashish believes that technology should be inclusive, intuitive, and infused with humanity. His writing invites readers to think critically, ask better questions, and embrace the future, not with fear, but with informed imagination.

www.ingramcontent.com/pod-product-compliance
Ingram Content Group UK Ltd.
Pitfield, Milton Keynes, MK11 3LW, UK
UKHW021409190726
13845UKWH00028B/981

9 789334 433036